On Solitude, Conscience, Love and Our Inner and Outer Lives

READING AUGUSTINE

Series Editor:

Miles Hollingworth

Reading Augustine offers personal and close readings of St. Augustine of Hippo from leading philosophers and religious scholars. Its aim is to make clear Augustine's importance to contemporary thought and to present Augustine not only or primarily as a pre-eminent Christian thinker but as a philosophical, spiritual, literary, and intellectual icon of the West.

Volumes in the series:

On Ethics, Politics and Psychology in the Twenty-First Century
John Rist

On Love, Confession, Surrender and the Moral Self
Ian Clausen

On Education, Formation, Citizenship and the Lost Purpose of Learning
Joseph Clair

On Creativity, Liberty, Love and the Beauty of the Law
Todd Breyfogle

On Consumer Culture, Identity, the Church and the Rhetorics of Delight (forthcoming)
Mark Clavier

On Self-Harm, Narcissism, Atonement and the Vulnerable Christ (forthcoming)
David Vincent Meconi

On God, the Soul, Evil and the Rise of Christianity (forthcoming)
John Peter Kenney

On Music, Sound, Affect and Ineffability (forthcoming)
Carol Harrison

On Solitude, Conscience, Love and Our Inner and Outer Lives

Ron Haflidson

LONDON • NEW YORK • OXFORD • NEW DELHI • SYDNEY

T&T CLARK
Bloomsbury Publishing Plc
50 Bedford Square, London, WC1B 3DP, UK
1385 Broadway, New York, NY 10018, USA

BLOOMSBURY, T&T CLARK and the T&T Clark logo are
trademarks of Bloomsbury Publishing Plc

First published in Great Britain 2019

Cover design: Terry Woodley
Cover image © Sam Germaine-Scrivens, Getty

A catalogue record for this book is available from the British Library.

A catalogue record for this book is available from the Library of Congress.

ISBN: HB: 978-0-5676-8268-0
        PB: 978-0-5676-8273-4
        ePDF: 978-0-5676-8269-7
        ePUB: 978-0-5676-8272-7

Series: Reading Augustine

Typeset by Integra Software Services Pvt. Ltd.
Printed and bound in Great Britain

To find out more about our authors and books visit www.bloomsbury.com
and sign up for our newsletters.

Dedicated in grateful memory to my mother,
Gwen Haflidson (1949–2015)

"Love … hopes all things, endures all things."
—1 Corinthians 13:14

CONTENTS

ACKNOWLEDGMENTS

My interest in theology and philosophy was cultivated and channeled at a formative stage in my life by Ruth and Jack McLaughlin. I was one of generations of grateful students from Northern Ontario who received a world-class education, thanks to these public high-school teachers. I am blessed to have studied Augustine under an eclectic (and consistently superb) group of scholars and teachers. Their variety of styles and perspectives heightened my sensitivity to the depths of Augustine's thinking; these include Colin Starnes, Robert Crouse, Wayne Hankey, Neil Robertson, Angus Johnston, Peter Widdicombe, Sarah Parvis, and Oliver O'Donovan. From that list, three deserve special mention. If it weren't for the typically wise and generous advice of Professor Widdicombe, I would have abandoned studying Augustine far too early. Some of the material in this book was first developed in my doctoral dissertation at the University of Edinburgh, where I was supervised by Oliver O'Donovan and Sarah Parvis. I am grateful to Professor O'Donovan for his unfailingly penetrating feedback on my work and to Dr. Parvis for her care throughout my time at Edinburgh.

A number of people kindly provided invaluable feedback on this project at various key stages of its development (including some who gave up precious summer days to read a whole draft); these include James Alison, Andre Barbera, Kerry Balden, Thomas Clement, Robert Druecker, Anthony Dupont, Rachel Goad, John Haflidson, Miles Hollingworth, Margaret Kirby, and Rachel Langston. The clarity of my thinking and quality of my writing (such as they are) improved dramatically because of the feedback I received from them.

I presented a version of the first chapter as a lecture in the Graduate Institute lecture series at St. John's College in Annapolis, Maryland, in June 2018. The students and faculty who attended the Question Period raised all sorts of great questions (appropriately enough) that challenged me to think more carefully than I had been about different kinds of solitude. I have benefited enormously from conversations about solitude (among other topics) with these St. John's colleagues: Robert Abbott, Andre Barbera, Karin Ekholm, Rebecca Goldner, and Zena Hitz. I regard it as one of the great blessings of my life to belong to a genuine intellectual community where searching and collaborative conversations happen on a daily basis.

My family, in typical fashion, have shown keen interest and provided unfailing support over the course of this project. I am grateful to my father, John Haflidson, for encouraging me—for as long as I can remember—to pursue my passions and take the risks necessary to do so. I can always depend on my sister, Kara Haflidson, for clearheaded advice and a good laugh. She is one of the wisest people I know. Finally, I absolutely must thank my partner, Tom Clement, who has had to put up with me as I wrote this book (and really should have been doing all sorts of other things). I am grateful to him for the myriad ways he is so constantly and consistently generous toward me—a generosity that reflects that of his "Father in heaven ... [who] sends rain on the just and unjust alike" (Matt. 5:45).

Introduction

I write this book out of the conviction that solitude is under threat in our day and that its decline and loss is dangerous for us. There is ample evidence that to achieve great things in a range of human endeavors solitude is necessary. For the novelist, the scientist, and the saint, time alone is required to do their respective work; time alone is not the only thing necessary, of course, but time alone does seem essential. As well, at long last, introverts lately have been receiving the attention they deserve (though may not want ...). For these people too, among whom I count myself, constant interaction with others is a drain, and so time alone is a condition for their survival. But my concern about the preservation of solitude in the contemporary world is not focused merely on introverts and the intellectually and spiritually ambitious, though it does include them. My concern is primarily with why solitude may be morally necessary for all of us. I believe there may be a vital connection between spending time alone and living a good life. And while I cannot offer a comprehensive definition of what a good life involves, I think it includes, at the very least, making some positive difference to this world during the short time we've got. If solitude is a means to that end, then its preservation is not a minority or esoteric interest at all.

A preliminary definition of solitude

Before proceeding to further outline the threat to solitude in our day, a working definition of solitude is in order. I hope that our understanding of solitude will be enriched and refined over the course of this inquiry, largely thanks to the thought of a fifth-century theologian, priest, and bishop, Saint Augustine, who will be our primary focus beginning in the second chapter. His thinking on solitude, in my view, has yet to reach its expiry date. I will save considering his particular approach to solitude until later. At this preliminary stage, let me define solitude as a state that supports certain activities. The state, at its most basic, is the lack of other human companions. Immediately, with this definition, the specter of loneliness appears, for it, too, consists in the lack of human companions. The difference is that with loneliness, we experience that lack as a gnawing absence that is devastating to our sense of self and our place in the world; whereas in solitude, that lack serves as a space to be filled. A variety of activities may serve to fill the space that opens up in solitude. They may include everything from attending to one's breath in meditation to contemplating the nature of truth, from idle daydreaming to going for a long walk. As we shall see shortly, often advocates for solitude point to the benefits of introspection, a catchall term that literally means "looking inside." Introspection takes a variety of forms, all of which are marked by attention to oneself; the focus of this book will be on the moral value of prayerful introspection, specifically engaging in a searching examination of who one is and how one lives one's life before God. So while I am sure there are benefits to other activities we may do in solitude, I will be considering how solitude may support this discipline of self-examination. In the first chapter, I will consider how the lack of human companions in solitude allows us to pursue the company of other companions: ourselves, nature, and God. Our introspection may take place under the influence of those companions who offer an alternate perspective from which to see ourselves. We will treat Augustine in the subsequent three chapters as an expert on the influence God's companionship may play in solitude.

The contemporary threats to solitude

Back to the threat to solitude in our own day. This concern is not original to me; it is a very old and recurring one, and this in itself may make it less credible. Perhaps fear about the loss of solitude belongs to curmudgeons of every age who compare the paucities of "these days" with the glories of "the good old days." I confess that I do have certain predispositions in the curmudgeonly direction. And so if squawking about solitude is confined to those who are interminably grumpy or nostalgic, we ought to be skeptical how urgent or important the concern is. What, if anything, sets our age apart in terms of the threat to solitude? And what do we risk losing if solitude is indeed under threat?

In this Introduction, I will explore the answers to these two questions offered by four contemporary authors. I have chosen these particular four because, despite their range of areas of expertise and different perspectives, they share the opinion that solitude is under threat and we ought to preserve it. And each makes a case for why we ought to preserve solitude on moral grounds. As well, the work of each of them has received attention, which seems to indicate that their concerns resonate. They are psychologist and sociologist Sherry Turkle; English scholar and critic William Deresiewicz; novelist Sarah Maitland; and memoirist and novelist Fenton Johnson. These are, we might say, leading members of a coalition for the preservation of solitude in the contemporary age. I will offer only snapshots of each of these thinkers' views on solitude; my purpose at this point is to dive into the contemporary conversation on solitude in order to get a sense of the questions and issues involved. After meeting these members of our coalition, I will describe how I hope to contribute to their work with this book and why Augustine's writings will be my main focus.

Our first question is why the threat to solitude today may be unprecedented. One essential part of the answer concerns the contemporary technological developments that make it possible to remain constantly connected to others. In what seems delightfully quaint today, Henry David Thoreau (to whom we shall return in the first chapter) was angry that even from his cabin in the woods he could hear the train's whistle, ensuring that the sounds of the civilization he was fleeing violated his solitude.[1] Perhaps all technological developments—from the printing press to the wheel— were met with similar complaints. Even so, what would Thoreau

---

[1] Henry David Thoreau, *Walden and Civil Disobedience* (1854; New York: Penguin Books, 1960), 82.

make of our world today, where a range of devices constantly flash and beep, often, if not in our hands, then in our pockets or very nearby, making it increasingly possible (and perhaps irresistible) to remain constantly connected to others? Whereas our lives previously would have been characterized by daily smatterings of solitude, most of the times and spaces where solitude arose have been filled with devices that keep us in constant contact with each other. The blessings of such contact are numerous and significant. Even so, our concern that solitude is endangered is justified by the unprecedented way in which these technologies pervade our everyday lives. Thoreau's train whistle is nothing compared to the onslaught of technologically mediated contact today.

The result of these technological innovations is that how we think of solitude has itself already undergone a worrying transformation. In her extensive interviews with teenagers and college students, Sherry Turkle often asks whether they regularly spend any time by themselves; for those who answer affirmatively, they most often refer to time spent by themselves while online.[2] Thus, as Turkle puts it, this contemporary wired solitude ensures that we find "*in solitude, new intimacies.*"[3] Such solitude, though, is not truly solitary, as one is definitely aware of being in human company. Solitude has now come to be defined, then, as the absence of *embodied* human company. Many members of younger generations have not experienced any alternatives to this wired solitude, and some cannot even fathom the possibility that time alone would be anything other than torture. Turkle concludes that this wired solitude is nothing but a "shadow" of the fuller sense of solitude.[4]

Turkle answers our second question, about what is under threat with the decline of solitude, in terms of the quality of our relationships with others. Constant connection, in her view, is not giving our relationships new depth. Instead, the people we engage with online become "personae ... reduced to their profiles," and

---

[2]Sherry Turkle, *Reclaiming Conversation: The Power of Talk in a Digital Age* (New York: Penguin Press, 2015), 74.
[3]Sherry Turkle, *Alone Together: Why We Expect More from Technology and Less from Each Other* (New York: Basic Books, 2011), 18.
[4]Turkle, *Reclaiming Conversation*, 163.

when we engage with people on our mobile devices we often do so while juggling several other online tasks and also, perhaps, walking or driving. These sorts of engagements do not foster genuine connection. So the other side of contemporary solitude is that "we are increasingly connected to each other but oddly more alone: *in intimacy, new solitudes.*"[5] The result, Turkle argues, is a "vicious circle":

> Afraid of being alone, we struggle to pay attention to ourselves. And what suffers is our ability to pay attention to each other. If we can't find our own center, we lose confidence in what we have to offer others. Or you can work the circle the other way: We struggle to pay attention to each other, and what suffers is our ability to know ourselves.[6]

Our capacity for compassion, among other things, is under threat. In the third chapter, we shall consider Augustine's analysis of this link between introspection and compassion.

While the technological threat to solitude is unprecedented, it is too easy to blame technology. Technological developments are the result of human intelligence and industry, and their success comes, at least in part, from human demand. Another reason, then, that the danger to solitude is especially great in our age is the relatively little cultural value we seem to place on it. So we ought also to consider the cultural influences at work that determine whether individuals, communities, and institutions are carving out times and places where solitude is available. We shall consider such influences (admittedly with very broad strokes).

English scholar and critic William Deresiewicz summarizes an overriding social momentum in terms of our "culture of connectivity." What the contemporary self wants above all, he argues, is "visibility."[7] When that is our priority, solitude is repellent; instead, to be a self depends on being constantly seen. Just as technologically our society may be unprecedented, so too our "culture of connectivity" stands

---

[5]Ibid., 19.
[6]Ibid., 11.
[7]William Deresiewicz, "The End of Solitude," *The Chronicle of Higher Education*, January 30, 2009, http://chronicle.com/article/The-End-Of-Solitude/3708.

out if we take a longer view. Deresiewicz offers a short, truncated overview of a millennia of history by dividing it into different ages according to the value each age placed on solitude. In his telling, each age also has its correspondent hero who depended on solitude. The variety of heroes Deresiewicz identifies—from the Buddhist guru in meditation to the Romantic poet off on a solitary walk, to name only two—demonstrates how, despite profound contrasts between cultures, in each case solitude was upheld as invaluable and space was made for it. As Deresiewicz puts it, in all these previous ages, the "examination of the self ... [is] placed at the center of spiritual life—of wisdom, of conduct."[8] In our own age, by contrast, our use of technology "seems to involve a constant effort to stave off the possibility of solitude, a continuous attempt, as we sit alone at our computers, to maintain the imaginative presence of others."[9] When our attention is so occupied with others, even if we aren't actively communicating with them, that prevents the "looking within" that defines introspection.

The loss of solitude, Deresiewicz believes, threatens our ability to be critical of ourselves and society. Time alone enables us, as Deresiewicz puts it, to "think one's way [beyond] society."[10] The cultivation of solitude can "protect oneself from the momentum of intellectual and moral consensus."[11] When you're alone, you can't depend on others to think for you, and so you have to think things through for yourself and to consider what your beliefs demand of you.[12] Solitude, then, is a means not only of discovering one's deepest convictions but also of developing the strength to stand up for them. In the second chapter, we shall take up this theme when we see how Augustine believes that a proper examination of conscience, by which we may gain a critical perspective on ourselves and the influences that shape us, demands solitude; and in the third chapter, we shall focus on how such an examination of conscience,

---

[8]Ibid.
[9]Ibid.
[10]Ibid.
[11]Ibid.
[12]For a practical application of Deresiewicz's account of solitude, see the text of his address to the United States Military Academy at West Point, entitled "Solitude and Leadership," *The American Scholar*, Spring 2010, http://www.theamericanscholar. org/solitude-and-leadership/print/.

for Augustine, involves an interrogation of how we love (or fail to love) others.

Another member of our contemporary coalition is Fenton Johnson, whose own analysis of contemporary culture complements Deresiewicz's characterization of a "culture of connectivity." Johnson provocatively suggests that our widespread discomfort with solitude may be the converse of our contemporary obsession with sex. While solitude does not necessarily imply celibacy, Johnson notes that for both religious and artistic solitaries the two often do go together. He thinks our obsession with sex belongs to a deeper discomfort contemporary culture reflects with freely chosen "discipline,"[13] what he even provocatively calls an "ascetic" life.[14] To refuse either human company or sexual intimacy, Johnson argues, is to choose to suffer from the lack of what are undoubtedly goods. In a culture that seems obsessed with choice, the minute one product does not instantly satisfy we drop it and try the next. This consumerist attitude is not confined to the shopping mall but permeates our way of life. Taking up a discipline, then, in which rewards may not be instantaneous, and things may continue to be difficult, is a decision that is counter to much of our cultural formation.

And yet, at the center of Johnson's essay is the claim that solitude and celibacy should not be understood primarily in terms of what one is losing but how those losses are necessary for other greater gains, namely "the deepening of the self, the interior journey."[15] In a culture that seems to be defined by a variety of excesses, and the crises that come from them, Johnson argues solitude is a countercultural practice that may make us more sensitive to the given riches of our existence. For proof of the rewards of this way of life, Johnson draws analogies between religious and artistic solitaries. Like religious celibates who give up sexual intimacy with one individual to turn their attention to communion with all, he describes how for artists "solitude was a vehicle for the imagination."[16] In their solitude, Johnson argues, they were able to

---

[13]Fenton Johnson, "Going It Alone: The Dignity and Challenge of Solitude," *Harper's Magazine*, April 2015: 34.

[14]Ibid., 33.

[15]Ibid., 34.

[16]Ibid., 39.

withdraw from the "background noise of society"[17] to commune instead "with the great silence, the great Alone."[18] By doing so, these solitaries had a heightened sense of what it means to be alive, both life's glories and its tragedies, and they could represent that to us in their art. Their asceticism, then, he writes, was an "opulent asceticism"[19]; the sacrifice of certain pleasures was the condition for an abundance of others. Like Turkle, Johnson suggests that solitude may heighten our compassion for others; and like Deresiewicz, he sees solitude forming us to be more critical, in particular to ask "an essential question, one that is more important now than ever, and is antithetical both to capitalism and to science as we practice them: Because we can do something, must we do it"?[20]

A final member of our coalition, Sarah Maitland, will serve to conclude this brief survey of contemporary authors. Maitland indicts modern Western culture for being oblivious to an obvious contradiction in the supposed priority we place on the individual. Through a combination of personal anecdotes and cultural analysis, in *How to Be Alone*, she summarizes depictions of modern-day solitaries as "sad, mad or bad." As her own experience of describing her life with others confirms, there is a widespread view that those who make time alone a priority are either depressed, mentally unwell, or immoral.[21] We might characterize one cause of this view as a confusion about the distinction between solitude and loneliness; certainly we are right to associate loneliness with the "sad, mad or bad," but what about solitude? Maitland's most bracing insight is not merely this cultural avoidance of solitude; instead, she believes this avoidance points to a hypocrisy in our supposed treasuring of individuality. On the one hand, she notes, we value, perhaps more than ever before, "autonomy, personal freedom, fulfillment and human rights, and above all individual freedom," and yet these same supposedly liberated individuals are "terrified of being alone with themselves."[22] What is at stake in the decline of solitude, then, is our

---

[17]Ibid.
[18]Ibid., 33.
[19]Ibid., 39.
[20]Ibid., 37.
[21]Sarah Maitland, *How to Be Alone* (London: MacMillan, 2014), 20.
[22]Ibid., 19–20.

very understanding of the individual. How truly individual are we if we are in constant flight from any time where we are genuinely alone with ourselves? Might not our discomfort with solitude, then, actually call into question the priority we place on individuality?

With the assistance of this coalition for the preservation of solitude, I hope we now might see clearly why the threat to solitude in our age may be especially grave. It is not only that our gadgets are more powerful and irresistible than ever before, though that certainly seems indisputable. It is also that, in broad strokes, currents in contemporary Western culture place little or no value on solitude. Solitude has already been redefined, according to Turkle, in terms of time alone online, though such constant connection compromises both our sense of ourselves and our relationships with others. Deresiewicz thinks that our contemporary conception of self prioritizes being seen by others, unlike in other eras, in which introspection was seen as essential for cultivating a critical perspective on oneself and society at large. Johnson identifies a pervasive consumer culture in which we are unable to commit ourselves to a long-term discipline that limits our choices and does not offer instantaneous satisfaction. Maitland accuses contemporary society of a gaping contradiction in our supposed affirmation of individuality because of how our society tends to neglect or even dismiss an individual's need for solitude.

Our authors also all agree that in giving up solitude we risk abandoning one vital means of moral formation. This may be represented by an image used by Michael Harris, a member of this coalition for the preservation of solitude himself, who asks us to consider solitude as a natural resource[23] that

> we can either nurture or allow to be depleted. Think of a forest. For centuries we could walk among dense stands of firs when we

---

[23]The metaphor of solitude as a resource assumes that it is a means to an end rather than an end in itself. I argue throughout this book that solitude is a valuable means to support the end of moral self-criticism; as I discuss briefly in the first chapter, other crucial approaches to solitude take solitude as an end in itself, as with certain practices of prayer and meditation. In the latter case, Harris's description of solitude as a natural resource would be inappropriate. He seems to assume that solitude is ever only a means to an end. I am grateful to my colleague Margaret Kirby for alerting me to this assumption in Harris's metaphor.

chose, or profit from cutting the same trees down without much care as to whether nature at large would be materially damaged. Then a line was crossed and we found ourselves starved for green space ... Solitude is consumed and depleted as surely as Brazilian rainforests are toppled and the tar sands of Alberta are sucked dry. This is how we make an Easter Island of the mind.[24]

If our coalition is right, solitude is not only necessary for those aspiring to some lofty accomplishment or another but may be a valuable resource in the living of a good life—which is, I take it, a more common, if no less challenging, aspiration. Turkle fears that online connections lack depth and that constant sociality actually weakens our capacity for compassion by squandering the time spent in introspection that develops our sense of self. Deresiewicz sees evidence that without time alone we are more likely to go along with the majority, instead of standing up for what we know is right. Johnson believes that the excesses of our contemporary culture are numbing us to each other and to the fragility of our world, and so we need a band of people committed to solitude to show forth an alternative way of seeing and living in the world. Maitland regards our culture's supposed valuing of the individual as fundamentally incoherent given our general neglect of solitude. Thus while it may seem that given all the other challenges we face, preserving solitude is little more than a quirky lifestyle choice, if these authors are right, a practice of solitude may support us to better face those very challenges.

The purpose of this book

In this book, I want to add my own voice to this coalition and do what I can to strengthen its arguments and so add to its persuasive force. I find each of these authors' arguments insightful and inspiring. Even so, I think our coalition has more work to do. In order to build a coalition for the preservation of solitude, these authors

---

[24]Michael Harris, *Solitude: In Pursuit of a Singular Life in a Crowded World* (New York: Thomas Dunne Books, 2017), 228–229.

reflect a pragmatic focus on what proponents of solitude share, and their association is solidified by some common enemies. Given the threat that solitude is under, this is an understandable choice. To borrow Harris's metaphor again, when the forest is nearly extinct, we need more than tree huggers to rally to protect it. Thus our authors focus on a dizzying array of characters (and convictions) who have demonstrated the necessity of solitude, from Buddha and Jesus to Jane Austen, Friedrich Nietzsche, and Walt Whitman. That this array all agree on the necessity of solitude has undoubted rhetorical force, given that they don't agree on much. In addition, our authors also tend to speak of solitude in a rather abstract way, as a catchall term that encompasses a wealth of different practices, from meditation to novel-writing. In their admirable desire to amass a coalition to preserve this precious resource, in other words, they are necessarily general and abstract. In particular, I fear that often religious and philosophical commitments that may make a fundamental difference to how one approaches solitude are treated as secondary, perhaps even incidental. I do not intend this criticism to be mere tedious, scholarly nit-picking. I think acknowledging and more fully exploring different approaches to solitude can serve to enrich this discussion and widen the contemporary experimentation that is possible.

In particular, I believe that it may make a distinct difference to how one understands solitude whether one believes in God or not; and if one does believe, what kind of a God it is. If one believes, as Jews, Christians, and Muslims do, that God creates all things from nothing, then certain things follow from identifying human beings as creatures dependent on a Creator. For one thing, as philosopher Thomas Prufer intriguingly puts it: "nothing creaturely *is* secretly (creaturely to be is to be displayed)."[25] If there is an omniscient and omnipotent God who created all things, in other words, then I am always known, and thus my solitude is never entirely solitary.

A way of articulating how "nothing creaturely *is* secretly" is in terms of the metaphor of God seeing us. This metaphor is prevalent in both the Hebrew Bible and the New Testament, including

---

[25]Thomas Prufer, "Creation, Solitude and Publicity," in *Recapitulations: Essays in Philosophy* (Washington, DC: Catholic University of America Press, 1993), 33. I am grateful to my colleague Michael Dink for recommending this essay to me.

the teachings of Jesus in the Gospel of Matthew, which we will consider in the next chapter. I refer to God's seeing as a metaphor because it attributes a physical sense to God and so is an obvious anthropomorphism. So as is the case with all metaphors (especially when the nature of God is at issue) it is partial. Further, to refer to God's "seeing" pictures God as a witness, separate from the one who is being observed, which does conform to belief in an all-knowing God; however, "seeing" also downplays a rich variety of ways in which God may not be separate from us at all, instead God is united with each one of us and at work in and through us; to capture the latter mode of God's presence, the metaphor of God's seeing needs to be balanced with other metaphors, like the one I just used of "union." Even as I acknowledge these limitations of the metaphor of God's seeing, in this book I will explore some of the moral value this metaphor has been put to. This metaphor will be decisive for Augustine's treatment of solitude.

Friedrich Nietzsche, devoted to sniffing out any and all whiffs of God's lingering influence, distinguished sharply between true solitude and its pious pretenders according to this metaphor. In *The Gay Science*, he writes: "Everything that is thought, written, painted, composed, even built and sculpted, belongs either to monologue art or to art before witnesses."[26] Monologue art refers to the best art, which is done in solitude; the self is alone, conferring only with himself. For those with faith, Nietzsche judges that this is only "seemingly monologue"; he writes, "for solitude does not yet exist to the pious—this invention was first made by us, the godless." The one with faith, even when alone, continues to evaluate his work "from the eye of the witness," whether it be God or some audience or other. This is fundamental to an "artist's entire optics."[27] It is only once the death of God is fully acknowledged and its implications absorbed, for Nietzsche, that the possibility of genuine solitude will exist. And only with such solitude, will it finally be possible to create ourselves and our values.

By contrast, as we shall see in the second and third chapters, Augustine contends that genuine solitude requires intentionally

---

[26]Nietzsche, *The Gay Science*, trans. Josefine Nauckhoff (1882; Cambridge: Cambridge University Press, 2001), 231–232.
[27]Ibid.

bringing oneself alone before God, to consider how God sees one. The "looking inside" of introspection, in other words, may be used to attune oneself to God's looking at oneself and others. This dynamic already may distinguish the solitude of faith from other solitudes because introspection is ultimately self-subverting; the turn toward the self may yield an opening to One who is beyond the self. When in her solitude the believer reflects on God's seeing of her, she may a discern a gap between her seeing and a more complete seeing—complete in terms of both its comprehensiveness and its compassion. The moral work of searching self-criticism is supported by this way of describing God's presence. Yet for Augustine God is not only a witness to our solitude but also an interlocutor within it. So, for Augustine, a primary use of solitude is to examine oneself in dialogue with and before God. This includes the role of conscience, which we will discuss at length.

Final introductory comments

Before I bring this Introduction to a close, there are a few more preliminary matters I should address: first, the origin of my interest in solitude; second, why Augustine is an appropriate focus to explore this topic; third, whom I see as my intended audience; fourth, an overview of the chapters; and, finally, the significance of the dedication.

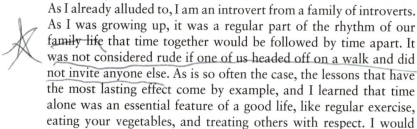
First, my interest in solitude comes from a number of influences. As I already alluded to, I am an introvert from a family of introverts. As I was growing up, it was a regular part of the rhythm of our family life that time together would be followed by time apart. It was not considered rude if one of us headed off on a walk and did not invite anyone else. As is so often the case, the lessons that have the most lasting effect come by example, and I learned that time alone was an essential feature of a good life, like regular exercise, eating your vegetables, and treating others with respect. I would further add that the moral worth of solitude came into clearer focus for me as I gradually admitted to myself that I was gay. As a teenager I feared disappointing those I loved and being rejected because of my sexuality. And as a Christian, and as a member of a Christian tradition that was (and is) involved in divisive and often

toxic debates about the morality of homosexual relationships, time alone became necessary for me to retreat from the debate and the fear of disappointment, to wrestle—for myself, alone before God—with who I was and how I was going to live my life.

Second, there is a wealth of authors with wisdom on the value of solitude. In this Introduction, we have considered some contemporary voices, and in the next chapter we shall consider other thinkers from the past century and earlier. And, as I detail further below, literary depictions of solitude will be consulted throughout. But our main focus, after the first chapter, will be on Augustine. What first attracted me to Augustine when I read *Confessions* in my first year of university, and what continues to bring me back to him, is the ever-present sense that he was a person of remarkable intellect and boundless passion who was committed to an honest and searching investigation for truth. He took his time converting to Christianity, trying out a variety of other options that were on offer. Once he had converted, living as he did in a formative period for Christianity, he fast became a well-known public intellectual, regularly responding to (and being dragged into) the leading debates of the day. Because of his own lengthy and tumultuous journey to faith and the debates that shaped his career in the church, Augustine did not come by his views easily; and he remained willing, throughout his life, to think things through again from the ground up. While I am an admirer of his—it may even be accurate to say I'm a fan—I also have my fair share of disagreements with him (though I have no doubt, if we were to ever find ourselves in a debate, he could wipe the floor with me). His writings on solitude, along with a list of other topics, I find marvelously and inimitably illuminating. So he has, in short, earned my trust as a guide on this topic, and I write this book in the expectation that what he has to say may be of use to others too.

I also ought to pause to stress that Augustine did not think that solitude is the answer to all our problems. Instead, Augustine has persuaded me that solitude is one practice among many that help to make up a good human life. For Augustine, solitude and community, especially the community of the church, are both necessary for us and should be mutually supporting and mutually enriching. To his mind, a Christian practice of solitude depends on the faith taught by the church and the worship that Christians share together. And, as we shall consider later, Augustine believed that solitude is only temporarily necessary as an interim measure, as the ultimate

Christian hope is that God will usher in a new creation in which we enjoy uninterrupted communion with God and each other.

Third, one of the constant pieces of advice given to authors is to get clear in your mind the audience you are writing for. I have regularly found myself imagining my desired readers as a selection of my favorite students. While the students I have encountered are a self-selecting group, given that they chose to study in programs that require them to read a lot of big, old books, I have been relentlessly inspired by their search for wisdom and their own ongoing experiments with living justly. With them in mind, I have done my best to offer an exploration of solitude that is intellectually substantial, but my primary purpose is not to stake out a particular position in scholarly debate or to demonstrate my mastery of the literature on Augustine. Portions of this book were originally written as part of my doctoral thesis, so my thinking is certainly informed by many scholars' work; key influences will be referred to in the body of this work, while others will be reserved for the footnotes. And while I do think I make some contributions to the scholarly understanding of Augustine, I have done my best to bring up scholarly discussions only when it helps to better explicate what I think Augustine has to teach us about solitude. In short, I am writing for those who, like my students, are in search of truth that can help to orient them in their thinking and living, and are likely to get impatient if I am constantly surveying scholarly discussion or defending my own interpretations.

Fourth, let me now offer a fuller overview of this book. In the first chapter, we begin by developing a framework by which to distinguish different approaches to solitude in order to identify what may distinguish a faith-based solitude from other alternatives. In that chapter, our exploration will be wide-ranging and involves a number of different authors. In subsequent chapters, our focus will narrow primarily to Augustine, with regular references to literary depictions of solitude that, I hope, will both anchor things in the stories of particular lives and demonstrate how Augustine's thoughts on solitude have wider resonance. I will now describe each chapter in more detail.

In the first chapter ("Solitude and Its Companions"), I offer a framework to distinguish different approaches to solitude in terms of different companions that may be sought in solitude. Rather than seeing solitude as solitary, we can better understand its benefits—

especially moral benefits—by approaching solitude in terms of companionship. In this chapter we shall consider three companions sought in solitude and the kind of influence they offer: oneself, nature, and God. Each companion offers an alternative perspective on oneself that supports the work of self-criticism. In particular, I explore the cases made for solitude by Hannah Arendt, George Eliot, Henry David Thoreau, and Jesus of Nazareth. Jesus's practice of, and teaching about, solitude is a primary focus of the chapter.

In the second chapter ("The Privacy of Conscience"), we turn to Augustine as an inheritor and interpreter of Jesus's teaching on solitude. Augustine's understanding of the nature and role of conscience as an inner space in which we dwell alone before God allows an alternative viewpoint on one's actions. The primary purpose of this chapter is to examine Augustine's case for the difference such a practice of solitude in conscience can make on how we see ourselves and how it may facilitate a more rigorous self-criticism, while also offering strength to resist the destructive effects of shame. We shall briefly consult Jane Austen's literary depiction of conscience in *Mansfield Park*.

Having treated conscience as a place of solitude in the second chapter, in the third chapter ("The Publicity of Love") we reconnect that private inner space with our public life in the world. Augustine's focus on our inner lives is not about a decisive turn away from the world because for him a practice of solitude supports our love of each other. As in Jesus's teaching, then, for Augustine, the Christian practice of solitude is not finally antisocial, instead it is a means of resocializing us to love better in public. The work of self-criticism before God better prepares us to love our neighbors as ourselves. I detail a number of ways Augustine believes this is the case and also consider another enticing depiction of the relation between solitude and love in Marilynne Robinson's novel *Gilead*.

In the final chapter ("The Flight from Solitude"), we return to the question of why so many of us tend to avoid or even flee from solitude. Augustine's definition of pride as love of one's own power diagnoses one possible reason. Love of our own power has a relentless momentum that keeps us busy acting outwardly in the world and so prevents us from turning inward to examine ourselves before God. Augustine identifies three kinds of busyness following a triad of sins described in 1 John 2:15-16: the desire for physical pleasure, stimulation, and domination of others. In addition to keeping us busy acting in the world, these kinds of busyness also involve a failure to recognize our given limits, one possible ground for our self-examination. To spend time alone at all, especially time alone in which we bring ourselves before God, runs counter to the momentum of pride. An especially satisfying form this busyness can take is in judging others. Augustine's analysis of judging others will be discussed in relation to George Saunders's short story "Puppy."

Finally, let me end this Introduction with a word about the dedication. This book is dedicated to my mother because she lived, in her quiet way, a remarkable life, and while I never asked her outright, I expect solitude had something to do with it. Beset by a number of tragedies, including losing both her parents at a young age and then spending the last decade of her life battling cancer, she nonetheless lived a life marked by unwavering compassion for others and a relentless joy in the good things of life. There are no doubt myriad reasons she persevered so remarkably: strength of character, deep faith, fiercely supportive family and friends, a devoted and loving husband—the list could go on. I also suspect that a practice of solitude may have made a difference. She regularly went off on walks alone in her neighborhood, in the woods, and on the golf course, and when there was enough snow (which there often was in Northern Ontario), on her cross-country skis. I believe that the companionship of nature and God that she enjoyed in her solitude may have contributed some to her admirable life. So, while I don't think she ever read a word by Augustine, and she likely would have found much of his writings (and mine) tedious or irrelevant, I nonetheless think it is entirely appropriate to dedicate this book to her, in gratitude for her life.

1

Solitude and Its Companions

In the Introduction, I defined solitude as a state in which the absence of other human companions frees us up for other things, including introspection; among a variety of modes of introspection, the focus of this book is on self-examination, a crucial activity in our ongoing moral formation. I do not mean that solitude alone can make us more self-critical, but it is one of a range of practices that may help, others of which depend on others' company for conversation, counsel, and debate. In this chapter, I want to explore the relation between self-criticism and solitude in terms of alternative companions we may seek in solitude. This approach will offer a framework by which to compare different approaches to solitude. Rather than seeing solitude as solitary, then, despite the clear etymological basis for that association, in this chapter we shall consider how solitude may involve companions. While solitude always includes the lack of other people's companionship, that lack is a space that may be filled by three other companions: oneself, nature, and God. The influence of each one provides a different way of seeing oneself and so supports a more searching self-criticism. And when it comes to the companionship of God in solitude, as we shall see, Jesus instructs his followers to attune themselves most to God's seeing of them. The nature and effects of God's companionship will be a special focus of Augustine's understanding of solitude, which we will turn to in subsequent chapters.

I now want to offer a more extended definition of solitude than the one given in the Introduction. To state it negatively, solitude denotes the absence of all forms of direct or indirect human companionship, aside from ones' own company and how one may make others present by memory or imagination. One positive potential of the lack of other human companions is it provides an opportunity to pursue other kinds of companionship that offer an alternative perspective on oneself. Essential to this definition is how in solitude one is not receiving any direct communications from other human beings, whether face-to-face or through words or other means, but one is left to oneself. We may still be occupied with others when alone, as memories of others or imaginary conversations, for example, may unfold with remarkable force, yet these originate (at least most immediately) from oneself. I want to reserve solitude, then, for periods when we are not actively receiving any communication from other human beings but are left to ourselves as the only human immediately present, even if, when left to ourselves, we spend much of the time ruminating over what others have communicated or done when we were in their company. To illustrate with a metaphor: after a walk on the beach collecting an exciting assortment of shells and rocks, solitude is that period where you head home to inspect what you've gathered.[1] There is a distinction, in other words, between the taking in of a variety of influences when in others' companionship and the process of taking stock of those influences when on your own. I am not assuming that we need solitude only because others' influence on us is negative; whether others' influence is positive, negative, or somewhere in-between, I argue that time in solitude helps us to evaluate and negotiate the range of influences at work on us.

This definition means that reading is not a form of solitude. Reading is one means by which another is present to me, and it can often be an especially intimate and influential form of human companionship. I have fallen in love with authors from reading their words, and the arguments they make and the worlds they construct are an influence on me. I know my experience is far from singular, which leads me to believe that in reading we are receiving a communication. Yet even though I do not think reading is a form of solitude, I do think great books often provoke or even demand solitude, when we have to set the book down for a while and ponder what is being said or what has occurred; and the ideas, characters,

---

[1] I am grateful to my former student Rachel Goad for providing me with this metaphor.

and worlds that we first encounter in books may take up residence in us and be somehow present to us in our solitude as influences—perhaps even authorities—that we consult and contend with. Let me also add some qualifications regarding this framework of the three companions in solitude. First, I make no claim that it is the best or only way to distinguish different approaches to solitude. I hope it will be useful to illuminate some of the fundamental differences at work in diverse approaches to solitude. As I argued in the Introduction, many who have written about solitude recently tend to minimize or neglect such differences. Such authors have taken a general approach and by doing so have succeeded in showing that our age may be singular in the relatively little value it places on solitude. If we are now persuaded, as I am, that we need to re-consider the value of solitude for our age and work for its preservation, then we would do well to engage in a more sustained way with particular approaches to solitude. And, as I suggested earlier, surely we would expect that a practice of solitude that is suffused by faith in an ever-present God would differ in some marked ways from other kinds of solitude. So we will give the most attention in this chapter to Jesus's practice of, and teaching about, solitude as recorded in the New Testament gospels.

The second qualification is to underline how this is one narrow angle to take on solitude. Our focus on self-criticism—a key task of the moral life—involves a heightening of our self-consciousness. When I examine myself, I take my life up as a task, and I consider myself (my thinking and doing and feeling) as an object of scrutiny. This practice of solitude depends, then, on a heightening of self-consciousness, as we shall consider further below. Other practices of solitude involve not a heightening of self-consciousness but a lessening or falling away of it. To use one's solitude to meditate, for example, might involve forgetting about oneself for a while as you attend instead to your breath. So too a roughly analogous state may arise when alone in nature or in prayer to God; at such times, my "I" is not at the forefront of my attention, but I am occupied instead by some "other," say the wonder of a spider's web or gratitude toward God. To forget about myself for a while can come as a welcome relief, and it undoubtedly has moral benefits too. I take it that the popularity of meditation and mindfulness come, in part, from the value of this lessening or falling away of our self-consciousness. My focus on a practice of solitude that involves the heightening of self-consciousness is not meant to dismiss or denigrate practices of solitude that have an alternative aim. I think that a variety of practices of solitude complement one another; they certainly have in my life.[2] I am focusing on solitude for self-examination so that we might explore it in some depth.

The third qualification regarding this framework is that the boundaries between these three companions are not absolute. Instead I will be distinguishing these three approaches in terms of the *primary* companion that is sought in solitude. For some, seeking God's companionship is not a live option, as they may not believe in God or may believe in a God who is not accessible for companionship in any way. Alternately, God's companionship may be sought for first and foremost through companionship in nature; or God's companionship may be sought for through nature among other means. We can see already that the boundaries between these kinds of solitude may be permeable. This is especially the case given that all who uphold solitude as a vital practice, as far as I know, do so because it facilitates self-knowledge; even if, in other words, the primary companion one seeks is God or nature, inevitably one's own companionship is involved too—and self-knowledge comes because I may see myself differently with another companion's influence. At the very least, for heuristic purposes, we may imagine walls between our three different kinds of solitude, but walls with at least a large window and perhaps even a door. The image of a window is especially apt because a primary focus of this book is how a practice of solitude may help us to see ourselves and others differently.

Solitude in one's own company: George Eliot and Hannah Arendt

In the first kind of solitude, one may become more self-critical by entering into dialogue with oneself. In the company of other human

---

[2] I have in mind especially the Christian practice of prayer referred to as "contemplation." On this subject, I recommend especially Martin Laird, *Into the Silent Land: The Christian Practice of Contemplation* (Oxford: Oxford University Press, 2006).

companions, our attention is on them; and our sense of ourselves, often in ways that we may be largely unconscious of, is also bound up with our sense of ourselves in their presence. To seek one's own companionship in solitude is to free oneself up to focus on oneself and to take up oneself as a partner in conversation. Before we turn to Hannah Arendt's analysis of this kind of solitude, George Eliot's novel *Middlemarch* offers two concrete examples of what it looks like and the difference it can make.

Our first literary case study from *Middlemarch* is the priest Camden Farebrother. Thanks to the all-knowing point of view of the narrator, readers become spectators to one of Farebrother's moments of solitude, when he walks home after a discussion with one of his most adored parishioners, Mary Garth. The narrator informs us that while on his walk, Farebrother shrugged twice. This is the bodily expression of two key turning points in what the narrator calls his "inward dialogue" during his solitary walk. Following on from the conversation he had with Mary, Farebrother ponders whether Mary and an acquaintance of hers may have feelings for each other that go beyond friendship; he then immediately asks himself whether Mary may not be too good for this potential suitor. That question, we are told, prompts the first shrug. He then detects within himself a twinge of jealousy, given his profound affection for Mary. The second shrug comes from the admission that it is not plausible for him to get married.[3]

Another more extended internal dialogue forms a major turning point of *Middlemarch* and centers on its heroine, Dorothea Brooke. Having just encountered supposed evidence that a beloved friend has betrayed her, Dorothea retreats to her bedroom. This scene gives a play-by-play in which Dorothea's mood changes from overwhelming anger to a renewed commitment to others' well-being; an internal dialogue plays a pivotal role in effecting that change. First, there is an overflow of emotion that is released as she is "shaken by sobs" and the "fire" of her anger intensifies "in fitful returns of spurning reproach." Eventually, she is so exhausted that she falls asleep. Next, after she wakes, with her passions having lessened considerably, she engages in dialogue with herself: "she was no longer wrestling with her grief, but could sit down with it

---

[3]George Eliot, *Middlemarch* (1871; New York: The Modern Library, 2000), 390.

as a lasting companion and make it a sharer in her thoughts."[4] Her grief is personified as a companion with whom she is in dialogue. In particular, she imaginatively reviews the events of the previous day that had so devastated her, putting questions to herself that lead her to engage with others' points of view: "She began now to live through that yesterday morning deliberately again, forcing herself to dwell on every detail and its possible meaning. Was she alone in that scene? Was it her event only?"[5] This allows the sympathy that had initially motivated her to act, before she discovered the betrayal, to rise again, and she recommits herself to acting on this person's behalf. The conclusion of the scene indicates how Dorothea's long night results in the ability to look beyond herself: "There was light piercing into the room. She opened her curtains, and looked out towards the bit of road that lay in view, with fields beyond, outside the entrance-gates."[6] Her anger tried to persuade her that she was the center of the world and that she owed nothing to any who had hurt her or who were involved with those who hurt her. After some time in companionship with herself, a turn within, she is now better prepared to turn without. Rather than closing her within herself, then, Dorothea's self-criticism in solitude opened her up; her solitude prepares her to better look out the window.

These examples of solitude as companionship with oneself furnish us with several provisional conclusions about the potential benefits of this kind of solitude. In general, Eliot depicts solitude as one means of maturing out of what she refers to elsewhere in the novel as our universal "moral stupidity" in which we take "the world as an udder to feed our supreme selves."[7] Dialogue with oneself in solitude opens up a space to be critical of oneself, especially the innumerable ways in which our first-person perspective on the world often leads us to assume that everything and everyone else are at our service. To enter into dialogue with oneself about that first-person perspective is to step back from assuming one's view on the world, to instead intentionally call it into question and place it alongside others' views.

---

[4]Ibid., 750.
[5]Ibid.
[6]Ibid., 751.
[7]Ibid., 201.

How does solitude furnish us with unique circumstances to call into question our first-person perspective? First, solitude is a form of privacy that may facilitate honesty with oneself. Farebrother never admits to anyone else over the course of the novel that his feelings for Mary had a romantic side to them. Likewise, Dorothea had not previously acknowledged to herself the feelings she had for the friend who betrayed her. In addition, her raw, emotional outburst likely depended on her being alone. This is not to say that conversation with another human being might not also facilitate honesty and emotional release too, but solitude may be available to us when a trusted friend or professional guide is not.

Second, solitude gives one the freedom to narrowly focus one's attention on oneself. Our attention is finite, and in the company of others, our attention is at least partly engaged by them, as well it should be. When alone, we can choose to direct our attention as we wish, though this assumes, evidently, the self-discipline to slow down and concentrate. The moral possibilities of solitude will be squandered if we use such time to come up with our grocery list. Both Farebrother and Dorothea review recent encounters with others and narrow their focus to particular moments in those encounters so that they notice what they did not at the time. The form this takes for these two is a dialogue with themselves about themselves. In so doing they make of themselves an object for observation and interrogation that would generally not be possible with others present. The purpose for Eliot, though, is not to become further self-involved; instead it is to call into question one's initial interpretation of, and interactions with, others. As seen most clearly in the case of Dorothea, after she gains some clarity about what she is feeling, and she lets the intensity of her feelings subside, she deliberately questions whether her feeling is an appropriate response to what occurred, given the other people who were involved. So Dorothea's time in solitude eventually enables her to look out the window, indicating she has renewed her openness to the world beyond herself. Her self-criticism supported that opening.

Hannah Arendt also believed in the transformative potential of dialogue with oneself. Her exploration of solitude was provoked by what she regarded as the unprecedented potential for loneliness in the twentieth century and the devastating social and political consequences of that horrid condition. After extensive study of one of the key figures in Nazi Germany, and of the totalitarian governments of Nazi Germany and Stalinist Russia, she understood both in terms of loneliness. In her study of Adolph Eichmann, the Nazi bureaucrat, Arendt noticed above all a "manifest shallowness" that she characterized not as "stupidity, but thoughtlessness."[8] Because of this "shallowness" and "stupidity," Arendt did not think that the instrumental role he played in the Nazis' success could be attributed to "any deeper level of roots or motives."[9] She argued, instead, that it came from a thoughtlessness that was bred from loneliness, which is the opposite, she contends, of solitude (as we will consider further below). For her, loneliness is "the experience of not belonging to the world at all."[10] Whereas one does have a companion in solitude—oneself—the lonely person is "actually one, deserted by all others,"[11] including oneself. The lonely person, then, is shut off from engaging with others because he does not identify as a member of a shared world, so his thinking becomes narrowed to what seems logical and consistent from his isolated point of view. Such a person is drawn to rules not primarily because he regards the content of the rules as true or just but because having rules satisfies his need for a certain—narrowly defined—rigor.[12]

Ideological thinking is a sterling example of this lonely mind-set, for ideologies, in Arendt's analysis, "always assume that one idea is sufficient to explain everything in the development from the premise, and that no experience can teach anything."[13] The lonely person, in other words, who does not feel they belong to a common world, is not receptive to learning from the world and the people in it; instead, he learns what he needs to all alone and then rigidly applies some truth to everything and everyone. Whereas Dorothea's solitude supported her to see more clearly when she looked out her bedroom window, the lonely person's time alone warps his perspective on others. As Roger Berkowitz writes, for Arendt the

---

[8]Hannah Arendt, *The Life of the Mind, Volume One: Thinking* (New York: Harcourt Brace Jovanovich, 1977), 4.

[9]Ibid.

[10]Hannah Arendt, *The Origins of Totalitarianism*, 2nd edn (New York: Meridian Books, 1958), 477.

[11]Ibid.

[12]Arendt, *Life of the Mind*, 177.

[13]Arendt, *The Origins of Totalitarianism*, 470.

lonely person is "prone to embrace a coherent and stable world offered by ideological extremism."[14]

Arendt argues that the kind of dialogue we can have with ourselves in solitude is a bulwark against acceptance of ideological thinking. In solitude, she writes, "I am 'by myself', together with myself, and therefore two-in-one."[15] Whereas in company with others, they regard me and I tend to regard myself as a united individual, in solitude I can acknowledge and let loose the duality within me; I can intentionally facilitate this duality when I engage in dialogue with myself. This duality comes when we make ourselves—our thinking and feeling and acting—the object of our reflection and deliberation, as Farebrother does with his jealousy and Dorothea with her anger. This kind of duality is essential, argues Arendt, for thinking: "It is this *duality* of myself with myself that makes thinking a true activity, in which I am both the one who asks and the one who answers. Thinking can become dialectical and critical because it goes through this questioning and answering process."[16]

Arendt's characterization of solitude in terms of this dialogue helpfully identifies the potential power of introspection. When we withdraw and enter into dialogue with ourselves, we are rendered active and given an opportunity to interrogate what we and others think and do. When I demand in dialogue with myself that I provide both the questions and the answers, I see what justification I can provide for views I may hold, but have largely passively absorbed from others. And, most critically for Arendt, I am likely to very quickly discover that I do not have certain and coherent accounts for all that I think and do; there are tensions and contradictions within myself that the dialogue with myself can both disclose and engage. It is not as though the world fades entirely from view, as often in our dialogue with ourselves we imaginatively present others to ourselves and engage in conversation with them; yet, when we do so, even as we mimic what we expect another's response to us would be, by taking responsibility for doing that mimicking we are challenging

---

[14]Roger Berkowitz, "Solitude and the Activity of Thinking," in *Thinking in Dark Times: Hannah Arendt on Ethics and Politics*, ed. Roger Berkowitz, Jeffrey Katz, and Thomas Keenan (New York: Fordham University Press, 2010), 237.

[15]Arendt, *The Origins of Totalitarianism*, 476.

[16]Arendt, *The Life of the Mind*, 185.

ourselves to see what sense we can make of varying viewpoints. In the company of others we can rely on them to speak for themselves and to give an account of who they are and how they think; in their constant presence we never have to think through, for ourselves, what influence they may have on us and what justification there may be for their views. Arendt's contention is that with this practice of solitude, doubts and disagreements emerge, and the possibility of critique is essentially endless. The moral significance of solitude, then, is it immunizes us from simply going along with what others think and even with what we may think. To quote Berkowitz again, for Arendt a vibrant solitude is "secured from the unthinking habits, common opinions, and constraints of the social."[17]

Even so, Arendt is not arguing that individuals can survive or thrive apart from our fellow human beings. Above all, my identity as an individual depends, in Arendt's beautiful characterization, on "the trusting and trustworthy company of my equals."[18] The dialogue with myself in solitude, then, depends on a community. Only if I am trusted by others, do I trust myself when in dialogue with myself; further, Arendt argues that the trust we have in our senses and experiences comes from engaging with others' with whom we share a common world. I have my perceptions of the world confirmed by others, and so I am not left endlessly doubtful about what I learn from my senses. Thus we may say that community provides the infrastructure for solitude. Most importantly, we require others to temporarily resolve the divided self that we become in conversation with ourselves. To be called by name, and to be spoken to as an individual, is to be made whole again; if I were to forever engage in critical dialogue with myself in solitude, Arendt says I would be "always equivocal" and divided, never a singular individual. When I return to the world after a period of solitude, I am given again the coherent identity of a person with "the single voice of one unexchangeable person." Arendt calls this the "redeeming grace of companionship."[19] The weighty religious terms that Arendt uses to describe this reunification underlines just how essential it is to alternate between periods of solitude and periods of human company.

---

[17]Berkowitz, "Solitude and the Activity of Thinking," 239.
[18]Arendt, *The Origins of Totalitarianism*, 477.
[19]Ibid.

Both Eliot and Arendt helpfully elucidate the power of entering into dialogue with oneself, though they are concerned with different ends. In *Middlemarch*, solitude is used primarily to interrogate my first-person perspective, which is often shored up by my immediate emotional reactions to interactions with others; Farebrother's jealousy and Dorothea's anger both take for granted that they are the center of the world, and others' desires are secondary or even incidental. Solitude allows them to recognize this self-centeredness and to expose themselves to the influence of other emotions they have, like their compassion for others whose best interest was somewhat obscure in the fast paced give-and-take of conversation with them. While Arendt's analysis of solitude no doubt includes this kind of emotional interrogation, she is especially concerned with how time alone in dialogue with myself can unleash a ceaseless process of criticism, in which fundamental questions are brought up and wrestled with, weakening the hold that convention and consensus have on us.

Solitude in nature's company: Henry David Thoreau

Arendt makes it clear that she wants to justify the moral necessity for solitude without needing to rely on any particular metaphysical or philosophical commitments. Instead, the experience of thinking itself, available to all of us, should confirm the moral value of solitude. A result of this, as noted above, is that the influence we seek in solitude is our own—a critical capacity that may lie dormant if we are too busy with others. There is an otherness, she says, inherent to our consciousness, as I can make myself an object to myself. We could even refer to this as an immanent transcendence that offers a critical distance on myself and the influences that form me. By contrast, our next two kinds of solitude involve seeking the influence of a nonhuman other: transcendent companions, in other words, whose influence serves to offer another way of seeing oneself and thus engaging in self-criticism. With the second kind of companionship sought in solitude, we consider the influence of nature.

There are many possible texts we could ponder in order to explore solitude as a means of seeking the companionship of nature. Given his status as a hero in many contemporary treatments of solitude, and the searching moral quality of his writings, Henry David Thoreau's description of his experiment with solitude in *Walden* seems an appropriate choice. For Thoreau, nature forms us to be critical of ultimately stultifying or destructive habits that have hardened into societal consensus. If we spend time in nature, it invites us into an alternative way of seeing ourselves and so of being in the world. Time in nature with others can have some of these effects too, but Thoreau suggests that the influence of nature is far more pronounced and transformative if we cut ourselves off from other companions for a while.

We start with the bad news. Life in civilized society, writes Thoreau, inducts us into "routine and habit everywhere [that are] built on purely illusory foundations."[20] One particular example is clothing. Fashion's influence multiplies our need for the number and style of clothing, as we need different clothes for different places and occasions, and this is all constantly changing. As well, many of our first and often abiding judgments of others may have to do with what they're wearing. The result of the influence of fashion, Thoreau believes, is that appearance is more of a priority than our moral character: "I am sure that there is a greater anxiety, commonly, to have fashionable, or at least clean and unpatched clothes, than to have a sound conscience."[21] He criticizes these perverse priorities in which a new appearance is sought over moral transformation: "I say, beware of all enterprises that require new clothes, and not rather a new wearer of clothes. If there is not a new man, how can the new clothes be made to fit?"[22] This one example of civilized society's influence demonstrates how it distorts our sense of what is important and distances us from the vital sources of moral and spiritual renewal.

For Thoreau, seeking nature's companionship in solitude is the most effective means to counter society's corrupting influence. These

---

[20]Henry David Thoreau, *Walden and Civil Disobedience* (1854; New York: Penguin Books, 1960), 69.
[21]Ibid., 19.
[22]Ibid., 20.

famous words from *Walden* encapsulate the moral significance of nature's companionship: "I went to the woods because I wished to live deliberately, to front only the essential facts of life and see if I could not learn what it had to teach, and not, when I came to die, to discover that I had not lived."[23] Away from human company and the routines and institutions of society, Thoreau is forced to begin again, as it were, and so to live his life "deliberately"; the challenge of living a more self-sufficient life demands that he rigorously examine what he is doing and why, because he can't continue doing all that he did previously when it all depends on him; thus he is forced to dwell with and on the "essential facts of life." This challenge, in other words, facilitates a critique of oneself and societal influences.

Yet it is not only that abandoning the comforts of civilization forces Thoreau to re-examine what our everyday lives tend to assume; he also attributes a morally admirable character to nature that invites him to adopt its ways for himself. In his chapter "Solitude," he says he only once felt lonely and that was early on in his time at his cabin. Quickly, though, "in the midst of a gentle rain ... I was suddenly sensible of such sweet and beneficent society in Nature, in the very patterning of the drops, and in every sound and sight around my house, an infinite and unaccountable friendliness all at once like an atmosphere sustaining me."[24] I am struck by how the phrase "infinite and unaccountable friendliness" suggests Thoreau is experiencing companionship and a companionship that seems to graciously enfold him.

Tracing out Thoreau's other references to rain offers a way to further consider one example of nature's companionship. Whereas he notes that in society rain is often regarded as "drear or melancholy," he found that it enforced a leisure on him that was conducive to thinking.[25] During the rain, he would go inside to discover that "thoughts had time to take root and unfold themselves."[26] This description depicts thoughts as plants that are watered by the rain. Nature's companionship, in this way, values extended periods of thinking, which Thoreau thinks society often prevents or even

---

[23]Ibid., 66.
[24]Ibid., 92.
[25]Ibid.
[26]Ibid., 93.

makes impossible. The rhythm the rain brings to human life serves as a means of criticizing the deadening rhythms of society.

Thoreau also traces the variety of goods that rain serves, and in so doing he relates his own good to a wider horizon. This horizon serves as a means of self-criticism, because the human good is situated relative to the good of other creatures. Thus the rain, Thoreau notes, is good for his crops, but he quickly adds that even if it rains too much and destroys his crops, it would be good for the grass elsewhere. Following the work of the rain removes him from the center of his perspective. He sees, in other words, how rain is a companion to others, some of which directly serve his well-being and others of which do so more indirectly or even not at all.[27] In an extended passage about a loon, he also conveys a sense that rain has connections that he knows nothing of; this is represented in a humorous passage, as he describes how he consistently tried to catch up to a loon, and regularly when he got close the loon would cry out and rain would begin to fall: "I was impressed as if it were the prayer of the loon answered, and his god was angry with me; and so I left him disappearing far away."[28] Despite the hyperbole, Thoreau reflects a sense that rain may have a more intimate relation with other creatures than himself. As occurred when Dorothea and Farebrother spent time alone, Thoreau's solitude gains him some critical distance on his first-person perspective, as he now sees his good in relation to the good of some of rain's other companions.

The companionship of nature, then, allows Thoreau to gradually wean himself off of society's corrupting influence to adopt instead a rhythm and a sense of what is good that is more life-giving. It is not only that living alone demands he reevaluate societal convention; further, nature's friendliness supports him to abandon such conventions by replacing them with other, more life-giving ways of being. Compared to society, in Thoreau's view, the demands of nature are minimal, and the support it offers is endlessly renewing. I hope that we have seen, even with this short consideration of Thoreau, one example of how nature's company may serve to offer an alternative perspective that forms us to be more critical of ourselves and others. Much more could be said on this front, in

---

[27]Ibid., 92.
[28]Ibid., 158.

terms of both Thoreau's analysis and other exemplars of this kind of solitude. We move on, instead, to the focus of this book, solitude as a means of seeking God's company.

Solitude in God's company: Jesus of Nazareth

As we turn to the third kind of solitude, I first note that it does not necessarily exclude the other two kinds of solitude. Thoreau himself regarded the company of nature as the primary means to enjoy the companionship of God. He is not alone in this. Others who pursued the companionship of God would see it as one of a number of means of pursuing God's influence. Among a myriad of places to look, we might turn to the Psalms: "The heavens are telling the glory of God, / and the firmament proclaims his handiwork. / Day to day pours forth speech, / and night to night declares knowledge."[29] These famous words picture how nature communicates God's character and how time in creation exposes one to God's influence.

Most importantly for us is how the inner dialogue that characterizes companionship with oneself, our first kind of solitude, is not abandoned when we seek the companionship of God in solitude. The Psalms are instructive here too. They often exhort us, for example, to seek our own company in times of extreme distress. In Psalm 77, the psalmist rehearses his suffering: "My eye flows at night, it will not stop. / I refuse to be consoled."[30] We then have an explicit turn to conversation with himself: "To my own heart I speak, and my spirit inquires."[31] So too in Psalm 4, readers are given this advice when overcome with anger: "Quake and do not offend. / Speak in your hearts on your beds, and be still."[32] As Hebrew translator and scholar Robert Alter comments on these verses, "The

---

[29]Ps. 19:1–2.

[30]Ps. 77:3. For this and the next Psalm I am using Robert Alter's translation: *The Book of Psalms*, trans. and commentary by Robert Alter (New York: W.W. Norton & Company, 2007).

[31]Ps. 77:7, trans. Alter.

[32]Ps. 4:5, trans. Alter.

auditors of the poem are exhorted to tremble as an act of conscience that will dissuade them from acts of transgression, then commune with themselves in the solitude of their beds and speak no more. The verse thus moves from a state of troubled agitation ('quake') to silence at the end."[33] These verses and Alter's comment on them could serve as a description of Dorothea's long night. The psalmist turns to solitude in order to engage in dialogue with himself. And yet in these Psalms, God is constantly referred to: God's absence is lamented, his goodness praised, his assistance requested, and his past acts are remembered. Whereas the first kind of solitude was marked by duality, though a duality in which one could make others imaginatively present, with this third kind of solitude there is a third companion present. God is, at the very least, a witness to the dialogue that the believer has with herself and, perhaps, also an active participant somehow in it.

This role for God, as depicted in the Psalms specifically and evident in the Hebrew Bible more generally, shaped Jesus's practice of solitude, as recorded in the New Testament. Jesus will serve as our primary exemplar of solitude as companionship with God. Many contemporary authors, including those we considered in the Introduction, uphold Jesus as an exemplar of the practice of solitude, though generally without an extended consideration of what his solitude looked like or what he is recorded to have said about it. We shall look at both Jesus's own recorded practice of solitude in which he retreats from the crowds to pray (though often to be interrupted) and his teaching on solitude, which belongs to his reinterpretation of the Israelite law. In Jesus's practice and teaching, time alone with and before God in private is a means to gain a critical perspective on oneself that supports a different way of acting in public.

In the Gospels of Matthew, Mark, and Luke, Jesus is recorded as taking time alone to pray to God. All three of these texts share two crucial episodes of such solitude: Jesus's temptations in the wilderness immediately after his baptism and his prayer in the Garden of Gethsemane immediately before his crucifixion. In all three, Jesus pursues solitude at crucial moments in his life. In addition to these, Luke records three other instances of solitude, while Matthew and Mark each record only one other instance.

---

[33]Alter, *The Book of Psalms*, 10.

The Gospel of John does not include Jesus's temptations in the wilderness or his prayer in the Garden of Gethsemane, though there is one clear instance in which Jesus pursues solitude to get away from the crowd similar to the other three gospels. I will argue that despite differences in the gospels' depictions of Jesus's practice of solitude, they all agree on two key features: first, Jesus retreats from the company of the crowd in order to remove himself from their influence; and, second, he lets his solitude be interrupted—and even interrupts it himself—to care for others.

We begin, then, with the first moment of solitude recorded in Matthew, Mark, and Luke, Jesus's temptation in the wilderness. Following his baptism by John the Baptist, and immediately prior to assuming his ministry of teaching and healing, Jesus spends time alone in the wilderness for forty days, where he is tempted by Satan. We are able to see who Jesus is when he is utterly alone, stripped of all the goods that we usually depend on from regular meals to human companionship. As we also saw above, time alone is marked as a space of self-knowledge, when so much of what usually defines us is absent.

What is striking about Jesus's response to Satan's temptations is that he is the same person in public as he is in private. What he learns about himself in the wilderness is a confirmation of his identity that was announced by his Father at his baptism and will be evident throughout the rest of his ministry. After he was baptized by John, God says, "You are my Son, the Beloved; with you I am well pleased."[34] Two of the three gospels begin God's words with "You," conveying the sense that the Father is addressing his Son, indicating a kind of dialogue between Father and Son. Satan's temptations in the wilderness all seek to compromise Jesus's identity as a beloved Son of God.

The three gospels differ somewhat in the presentation of these temptations. Mark is typically sparse, as we are told only that Satan tempted Jesus.[35] In Matthew and Luke we are told of a triad of temptations and how Jesus in each case refused them and quoted Scripture to Satan in response.[36] Though the order of the

---

[34]Mk 1:11 and Lk. 3:22b; compare Mt. 3:17.
[35]Mk 1:12–13.
[36]Mt. 4:1–11 and Lk. 4:1–13.

temptations differs in these two gospels, the temptations themselves are the same: to turn stones into bread; to throw himself off of the roof of the temple and have angels save him; and to worship Satan in exchange for the kingdom of the world. That Satan has Jesus's distinctive identity in mind is confirmed by his preface to two of the three temptations: "If you are the Son of God ... "[37] With the third temptation Satan makes it explicit that he is trying to sever the relation between Father and Son, as he invites Jesus to worship Satan instead. In rejecting each of these, Jesus shows that even when utterly alone, he remains the beloved Son of God, who refuses to prove who he is on Satan's terms. His public persona is entirely consistent with his solitary self at every moment he submits to, and thus embodies, the influence of his Father. In this way, as we shall consider further below, a practice of solitude is not in opposition to life in community. The intention, as seen in Jesus, is the seamless integration of public and private.

The final instance in which Jesus seeks solitude, shared by the three gospels, is his prayer in the Garden of Gethsemane. We learn that Jesus's solitude includes honest, searching conversation with God.[38] This form of prayer is a defining feature of Augustine's spiritual life, as we shall see. Unlike the majority of other times in which Jesus prays alone, at Gethsemane we get to hear what he says: "Abba, Father, for you all things are possible; remove this cup from me; yet, not what I want, but what you want."[39] Addressing God as "Father" reveals the intimate relation Jesus has with God, an intimacy that is also evident in his honest admission that he does not want to be crucified. The gospels differ as to whether he prays this once, twice, or three times. The repetition indicates that Jesus is engaged in a genuine dialogue with God in which he is really wanting an answer. The dialogue with oneself that defines the first kind of solitude is present here too, albeit with the added belief that God is witness to, and potentially a participant in, that dialogue. In particular, Jesus seeks God's company in order to surrender himself to God's influence.

Jesus's solitude seems to include, then, a practice of dialogue with God. But does Jesus receive some sort of response from God

---

[37]Mt. 4:4, 4:6 and Lk. 4:3, 4:9.
[38]Mk 14:32–42; Mt. 26:36–46; Lk. 22:39–53.
[39]Mk 14:36, with slight variation in the other gospels.

to his agonized prayer in the Garden of Gethsemane? The three gospels differ on this question. In the Gospel of Luke, God responds immediately after Jesus prays only once by sending an angel who strengthens Jesus.[40] In Mark and Matthew, no such angel arrives, and Jesus repeats his prayer, and eventually seems forced to stop praying by the arrival of Judas.[41] In these gospels, the interspersing of Jesus's repeated prayer to God and his request to his disciples to stay awake and pray suggest that he keeps reaching out for support and he doesn't receive it. Jesus's sense of abandonment by God, which begins at Gethsemane, culminates in the crucifixion when Jesus cries out from the cross, "My God, my God, why have you forsaken me?"[42] For these two gospels, then, Gethsemane is an instance in which Jesus seeks solitude in God's company but must endure loneliness instead.[43]

We saw above that for Arendt loneliness occurs when a person does not share his own company. An analogous loneliness may apply to this third kind of solitude when God's companionship is sought but seems lacking. The experience of God's absence is described by a myriad of religious traditions, and the challenge of how to interpret that absence is a fraught theological issue and an often agonizing trial in a believer's life. For our purposes, I want only to underline how two of the gospels seem to depict Jesus as experiencing loneliness, enduring it, and coming out the other side. This conforms to the teaching of the New Testament and Christian tradition that Jesus suffers from the most devastating features of our human condition and yet persists out of love for humanity and God. Even so, the knotty truth is that even if one believes in God's constant companionship, it may not always be manifest in one's life, replaced instead by a sense of God's absence; and so, one may seek out solitude in order to enjoy God's companionship, but experience loneliness instead. In such cases, for the Christian, this loneliness may be interpreted in terms of the pattern of crucifixion and resurrection, in the hope that suffering will eventually give

---

[40]Lk. 22:43.
[41]Mt. 26:45–49 and Mk 14:41–45.
[42]Mt. 27:46 and Mk 15:34.
[43]I am grateful to my colleague Andre Barbera for challenging me to think further about the difference between loneliness and solitude.

way to new life. I, for one, appreciate the admirable realism about the highs and lows of spiritual life, which includes both solitude in God's company and the gnawing experience of loneliness when God seems absent.

Earlier in the gospels, Jesus's practice of solitude reflects the transformative effects of God's companionship, especially in terms of developing a critical perspective on others' influence. We can take Jesus's address to God in the Garden of Gethsemane as a paradigmatic instance of Jesus's solitude. Even when the narrator doesn't record his prayer, we can conclude it is possible that some of Jesus's time in solitude includes dialogue before and with God. In other examples of his solitude, we also see him withdraw from the crowds in order to escape their influence, most frequently in the Gospel of Luke. After his first miracles, when the crowds come to him for healing, "Jesus would withdraw to deserted places and pray."[44] In one case, when the crowd is angry and begins plotting against him because he healed on the Sabbath day, his response is especially revealing. After a night alone in prayer, he chooses his twelve disciples. In other words, after others' anger and the threat of violence loom, Jesus does not cower but takes another—bolder— step in his public ministry. As well, the choice of twelve disciples recalls the twelve tribes of Israel, and so despite the accusation that Jesus violated the Jewish practice of Sabbath-keeping, he reaffirms his understanding of himself as a leader of the Jews.[45] There is a similar instance in Mark: after prayer, Jesus decides not to stay where he was, despite the adoring crowds clamoring for him to stick around, but instead he moves on to the neighboring towns because he says "that is what I came out to do."[46] With both these examples, Jesus's time in solitude comes immediately before he acts contrary to the crowds' wishes. His prayer alone helps him to resist the crowds' influence and to continue instead to live out his identity as Messiah given him by God.

Luke even seems to suggest that Jesus's solitude may involve his critical examination of the crowds' perceptions of him. After the feeding of the five thousand, Jesus moves a short distance away

---

[44]Lk. 5:16.
[45]Lk. 6:12.
[46]Mk 1:38.

from the disciples and prays alone. He is far enough away that their presence does not bother him, but near enough that he can address them when he wants to. At one point, he emerges from his solitude to ask, "'Who do the crowds say that I am?'" The question that comes from his solitude concerns the crowds' perception of him; this very well may also be the subject of his prayerful dialogue before and with God. The disciples detail that the crowd has conflicting views about who Jesus is. After Peter responds correctly that Jesus is the Messiah, Jesus responds: "If any want to become my followers, let them deny themselves and take up their cross daily and follow me. For those who want to save their life will lose it, and those who lose their life for my sake will save it."[47] His clarification about how his followers must be prepared to deny themselves may offer a clue into his understanding of the crowds' perceptions of him: Jesus knows that the crowds may like him because he is a miracle-worker, while the necessity of his eventual suffering would be abhorrent to them. In his solitude, Jesus distinguishes between an identity he sees the crowds projecting onto him, as the Messiah who puts an end to suffering, and his identity as the Son of God, whose life will end in failure as a crucified criminal.

The most explicit instance of Jesus's practice of solitude in the Gospel of John parallels this scene in Luke. After the feeding of the five thousand, John says: "When Jesus realized that they were about to come and take him by force to make him king, he withdrew again to the mountain by himself."[48] After Jesus miraculously fed the crowd, they want him to be their king—and they don't seem to care if Jesus is willing or not. His withdrawal from them reflects an earlier statement about his suspicions of the crowds: "Many believed in Jesus because they saw the signs that he was doing. But Jesus on his part would not entrust himself to them, because he knew all people, and needed no one to testify about anyone; for he himself knew what was in everyone."[49] After the crowd finally find him in John, Jesus attempts to educate them about how to interpret the miraculous feeding. He does so in terms of what kind of bread they should be seeking. He argues, first, that he is

---

[47]Lk. 9:22.
[48]Jn 6:10.
[49]Jn 2:23b-25.

the bread that truly satisfies, and, second, he also foreshadows his crucifixion when he refers to his body and blood as food. These are theologically dense claims. For our purposes, what is most relevant is that, as in Luke, we see that in John, Jesus withdraws into solitude in order to remove himself from the influence of the crowd, who misunderstand his mission.

We now need to put together Jesus's repeated withdrawal from the crowds with his willingness to have his solitude interrupted. His solitude, we might say, is permeable. He removes himself from the crowd in order to better prepare himself to care for them. The gospels show that Jesus allows his solitude to be interrupted or he even interrupts it himself. In the Gospel of Matthew, his need for solitude is heightened by the fact that he has just heard that John the Baptist was killed. Even so, as Matthew records it, he is drawn out of his time alone to heal the sick because of his "compassion for them."[50] In the Gospel of Mark, having escaped the crowds and his disciples for some time in prayer, when he sees his disciples in their boat struggling because of the extreme wind, he joins them and stills the waters.[51] And similarly in the Gospel of John, Jesus decides to end his time alone when he walks on water to meet his disciples who are overwhelmed by a storm.[52] These are stirring pictures of Jesus's commitment to care for others and how his seeking of God's companionship is never at the expense of his compassion for others. Jesus's commitment serves to temper what is often a very negative picture of his followers. His withdrawal from them is not permanent; it is a temporary necessity, for sure, but Jesus's compassion for others always brings him back to them. A question to keep in mind, then, as we turn to consider Jesus's teaching on solitude, is: How might solitude serve to support one's relationships with others?

In the Gospel of Matthew, Jesus commends a practice of solitude to his followers. The logic of his teaching is the same as that of his own practice: only by retreating regularly to spend time alone in the company of God may one gain critical distance from others' influence and expose oneself more fully to God's influence. The final result of God's influence in solitude, though, is not antisocial;

---

[50]Mt. 14:14.
[51]Mk 6:30–34.
[52]Jn 6:16–21.

instead, Jesus indicates that solitude is a means of resocializing his followers to better reflect God's image and so build a different kind of community.

Jesus mentions solitude when discussing almsgiving, prayer, and fasting. He uses a metaphor here that was already discussed in the Introduction and will occupy us for the remainder of this book: God's seeing of us. In particular, he says that the latter three activities should all be done "in secret" before "your Father who sees in secret."[53] Why these three activities in particular? First, it is likely the case that if one wanted to earn a reputation for religious piety, performing these three activities in public would likely do much for your brand. Jesus is engaged in a critique of such piety. Second, Jesus clearly does not have in mind that all three of these activities may be done in solitude. It would be impossible to give charitably without at least some one knowing about it; instead, to do it primarily for "your Father who sees in secret" is to not do it for the sake of others' admiring gaze. So too, Jesus advises us, when fasting, not to make a big show about it, instead to do one's best not to draw attention to yourself: "put oil on your head and wash your face, so that your fasting may be seen not by others but by your Father."[54] With this activity, too, we want God alone to see, even if others may inevitably notice that something is up. (I understand, for example, that fasting may make one a tad cranky.)

The one practice for which Jesus advises literal solitude is prayer. Not only should it be done alone, but Jesus also says to "go into your room and shut the door."[55] James Alison notes that the Greek word for "room" here refers to what we might call the "storeroom," which would have been a small room in the middle of house, without windows, where food was kept to protect it as much as possible from extreme temperatures.[56] Jesus is recommending, in short, that our prayer be as solitary as we can make it. We are to withdraw, for a time, to a room with no windows.

---

[53]Mt. 6:4, 6:6, 6:18.

[54]Mt. 6:18.

[55]Mt. 6:6.

[56]James Alison, "Prayer: A Case Study in Mimetic Anthropology," http://www.jamesalison.co.uk/pdf/eng54.pdf.

By looking more closely at the words Jesus teaches his followers to pray, we see that solitary prayer is not a rejection of one's relations with others but a means of re-forming those relations. Having advocated carving out as much solitude as one can get when praying, it is striking that the first words Jesus has his followers pray are "Our Father." The solitary individual presents herself to God as a member of a "we." And the "Father" that follows "Our" identifies all human beings as siblings under God. This sense of "we" remains throughout the prayer as the subject is repeatedly described as "us"[57] and the requests that are made are for "our daily bread,"[58] "our debts," and "our debtors."[59] The whole prayer locates the person praying in relationship to God and fellow human beings. All of us are united in our dependence on God, for bringing the kingdom, supplying our needs, and granting us forgiveness. And the person praying identifies her needs for material and spiritual sustenance as shared with others. The prayer, then, repeatedly returns the one praying to acknowledge her own neediness before God, which she shares in common with all her fellow human beings. Jesus is using solitude, in other words, to nudge us to acknowledge the neediness that we might try to hide in others' company. Prayer, then, might form us to be more critical of our pretensions to invulnerability.

The lines on forgiveness are especially noteworthy for how they construe the relationships between the person praying, others, and God: "And forgive us our debts, as we also have forgiven our debtors."[60] To receive forgiveness from God without granting it to others is a wrong done to another human being in need, a wrong that amounts to a denial of one's own ongoing need for forgiveness. Thus in the solitude of prayer, these words identify the person praying as one whose neediness is shared with fellow human beings and who owes to others whatever good is received from God. The acknowledgment of one's own neediness before God in solitude, then, becomes a kind of hinge by which we are turned outward to be more generous in offering forgiveness to others. The purpose of praying alone before God, in short, is to practice being a different

---

[57]Mt. 6:11, 6:12, 6:13.
[58]Mt. 6:11.
[59]Mt. 6:12.
[60]Ibid.

kind of self in private in order that we might be more of that self in public. Acknowledging one's neediness alone before God may increase the possibility that that same neediness is the basis for solidarity with others in one's public life.

That Jesus's teaching on solitude is a means of resocializing his followers is further confirmed by his use of the term "reward." Jesus contrasts the hypocrites who give alms, pray, and fast in public as having "received their reward,"[61] whereas those who do so "secretly" for God's eyes alone will receive their reward from the Father "who sees in secret."[62] It is perhaps tempting to read the reward the hypocrites receive as damnation, if one is predisposed toward fire and brimstone. Yet the verb is in the past tense. Jesus is not warning them they will receive their reward but saying they have *already* received it. If you act for others' approval, in other words, you may frequently get what you want. Those who act secretly, though, are to look *forward* to receiving a reward from their Father: God, they are told, "will reward you."[63] Again, we might be inclined to interpret this reward in terms of the afterlife and so take it to be heaven. I think it much more likely that Jesus may include in the Lord's Prayer itself a description of the "reward" one should seek when he instructs his followers to pray, "'Your kingdom come. Your will be done, On earth as in heaven.'"[64] So another way in which prayer might serve to reform the one praying is by orienting her toward the truest reward, namely seeing the fulfillment of God's will on earth. Heaven is defined in these lines as a realm in which God's will is already done, but the one praying asks that this also occur here too. Matthew suggests that Jesus was acutely aware of how our desire for others' approval forms us as moral agents. We are constantly attentive to how others see us, so Jesus is inviting us to attend to God's seeing of us instead. One consequence of this attention to the view of others is that we act for the immediate rush of other's approval, as opposed to acting for God's approval, which comes through the in-breaking of God's will on earth.

---

[61] Mt. 6:2, 6:5, 6:16.
[62] Mt. 6:4, 6:6, 6:18. In my reading of 'reward' I am influenced by James Alison; see his "Prayer: A Case Study in Mimetic Anthropology," http://www. jamesalison. co.uk/pdf/eng54.pdf.
[63] Mt. 6:4, 6:6, 6:18.
[64] Mt. 6:10.

Jesus's discussion of "reward" in Matthew resonates with what he says about "glory" in the Gospel of John. While that term may have religious connotations for us, the literal meaning of the Greek word *doxa* is much more prosaic: opinion and others' opinions of one, or, in other words, reputation. We could take the following passage from John, in which Jesus addresses a crowd, as an explicit statement of why Jesus pursues solitude: "'I do not accept glory from human beings. But I know that you do not have the love of God in you. I have come in my Father's name, and you do not accept me ... How can you believe when you accept glory from one another and do not accept the glory from the one who alone is God?'"[65] Jesus baldly tells his listeners here that his sense of identity and purpose is not determined by them; he does not pursue their approval. Further, Jesus harshly diagnoses these listeners' failure to believe in him as a result of how their own identities and purposes are determined by others' approval. They inevitably succumb, in other words, to their particular tribes' consensus and are unable to break from them in order to respond appropriately to Jesus. By contrast, John depicts Jesus's capacity for rejecting what would gain him human beings' favor as coming from his singular focus on receiving glory from the Father: "If I glorify myself, my glory is nothing. It is my Father who glorifies me."[66] Jesus is willing to ignore and even rebel against the moral conventions of others in order to act for God's glory. Seeking glory from God, in other words, empowers him to critically distance himself from the influence of others, whose morality is bound up with seeking approval from each other.[67]

To return to the Gospel of Matthew, Jesus there suggests how the reward we seek will shape our interactions with others. To see this we need to return to the earlier references to "reward" in Matthew chapter five. Having just proclaimed to his followers that they are "blessed" when they are hated and persecuted for following Christ, Jesus says, "Rejoice and be glad for your reward is great in heaven, for in the same way they persecuted the prophets who were before

---

[65]Jn 5:39–45.
[66]Jn 8:54a.
[67]In this interpretation of the significance of "glory" in John, I follow James Alison, *Raising Abel: The Recovery of the Eschatological Imagination* (London: SPCK, 1997), 180–181.

you."[68] As well, after he commands his followers to love their enemies, he refers to "reward" again: "For if you love those who love you, what reward do you have?"[69] In the former verse, Jesus encourages those facing persecution by affirming that God rewards them, despite the lack of reward they may receive from others; whereas in the latter verse, those who love only those who love them do not receive a reward from God. To seek reward from God, in other words, forms Jesus's followers to endure persecution and love their enemies.

If we return to Matthew chapter six, having seen these two earlier instances of "reward" in chapter five, the use of that term in relation to almsgiving, prayer, and fasting may appear different. It's not that God is somehow more present in solitude. Instead, by doing these activities in secret, one practices acting not for others' approval but for God's. To act for God's sight frees me from the need of constantly looking to how others are perceiving me. So these solitary practices habituate one to seeking out a different form of approval. This seeking of God's approval first in private makes possible a different way of relating to others when one goes public. So, as was the case with the Lord's Prayer, solitude inculcates a different way of relating to others. Indeed, Jesus commands his followers to act in public, as they are to be "the light of the world"[70]: "No one after lighting a lamp puts it under the bushel basket, but on the lamp stand, and it gives light to all in the house. In the same way, let your light shine before others, so that they may see your good works and give glory to your Father in heaven."[71] To hide from publicity is the equivalent of putting a lamp under a basket; it contradicts the very function for which it exists.

To take God's character as the ultimate criterion as to how one acts facilitates a self-critical perspective that does not passively absorb societal convention or consensus, whether by following it or reacting against it. When Jesus instructs his followers to love their enemies, he says, "Love your enemies and pray for those who persecute you, so that you may be children of your Father in heaven;

---

[68]Mt. 5:11–12.
[69]Mt. 5:46.
[70]Mt. 5:14.
[71]Mt. 5:15–16.

for he makes his sun rise on the evil and on the good, and sends rain on the righteous and the unrighteous ... Be perfect, therefore, as your heavenly Father is perfect."[72] Being generous to those who hate you reflects the abundant, indiscriminate goodness of God. To flee persecution or not love one's enemies would vastly limit one's generosity; both of the latter reactions would be natural consequences of seeking others' approval. Jesus envisions for his followers, then, a generosity that is not defined, as Oliver O'Donovan writes, by "staying within the limits which public rationality sets." Instead, Jesus calls his followers to enact "an extravagant, unmeasured goodness, corresponding to God's own providential care, [which] defies the logic of public expectation."[73] We have seen that Jesus commends a practice of solitude as a means of critically rejecting public expectation, yet doing so with the public good ultimately in mind. Solitude and publicity, in other words, are not opposed to one another; in solitude, the follower of Christ exposes herself to God's influence, so that she might more fully image God's character in public. From the point of view of Jesus's followers, then, among whom we include Augustine, companionship in God's company is the highest kind of solitude. Time alone in God's company helps us to live out our vocation as images of God.

Conclusion

All three of these companions in solitude, then, exert an influence that fosters moral self-criticism. When the companion is myself, the dialogue I enter with myself places me and the influences that form me under scrutiny. In *Middlemarch*, this scrutiny concerns especially my first-person perspective, in which my initial emotional reactions when I am with others tend to reflect the assumption that I am at the center of the world. Within solitude, I can gain some distance from those emotions and expose them to interrogation with others' own individual perspectives and needs more clearly in view. For Arendt, it is the duality of self-consciousness, which comes alive most fully

---

[72]Mt. 5:44–45; 5:48.
[73]Oliver O'Donovan, *The Desire of the Nations: Rediscovering the Roots of Political Theology* (Cambridge: Cambridge University Press, 1996), 110.

in solitude, that makes for rigorous critique of myself and others' influences on me. Our tendency in the company of others, when we are treated as coherent individuals and present ourselves as such, is to downplay the contradictions and tensions that are ever present to our thinking. The critical dialogue that occurs in solitude serves to establish a constant distance between me and any consensus or trend. The moral value of this is that those who pursue solitude in their own company will not be susceptible to ideology, which sets out to squelch human individuality.

What sets companionship with myself apart from the other two kinds of solitude is that the critical influence comes from oneself, albeit by representing to oneself a variety of other people, real and imagined. Conversation with oneself realizes a potential we always have within us, but often lose in our constant contact with each other. By contrast, the companions in the other two kinds of solitude transcend a human perspective. For Thoreau, with time alone in solitude, nature refines one's sense of what is essential and so frees one from the often pointless and exhausting priorities that society hoists upon us. So too, Jesus seeks the influence of his Father to distance himself from the crowds' adoration or hatred of him and to expose himself instead to the Father as the model for his actions. Yet he also lets his solitude be interrupted, an indication that ultimately Jesus's purpose is to invite all to share the companionship that he enjoys with the Father. Jesus's practice of solitude was consistent with his teachings on the subject. Time alone in God's company is a means of resocializing Jesus's followers, so that they can acknowledge their dependence on God and their common neediness with others, and they can act for God's approval, rather than others. By so doing, their public lives are intended to reflect God's character, especially in terms of their generosity, which extends even to enemies. Solitude in God's company, in short, is a temporary measure intended to assist Jesus's followers in building a different kind of human community that depends on a critical relation to what might otherwise appear as inevitable or unavoidable features of our sociality.

As I said at the beginning of this chapter, I make no claims for the comprehensiveness of this framework of different kinds of solitude. Even so, I hope it has helped us to identify some fundamental differences between these different kinds and, in particular, a distinctive feature of Jesus's teaching on solitude: the metaphor of God's seeing. The moral necessity of solitude, in all cases, consists in how it can facilitate an alternative perspective—a different seeing—of ourselves and the influences that form us. Yet to seek out God's companionship for Jesus involves attending to a transcendent seeing. Such a transcendent perspective does not seem possible through the company of oneself or nature. While there are many other examples we could turn to of these three companions that may be sought in solitude, it seems to me unlikely that companionship with oneself or nature would involve belief in such a transcendent seeing.

For the remainder of this book, we shall stay with this metaphor of God's sight to explore solitude in God's company. As a beginning of that exploration, Rowan Williams draws an intriguing connection between aesthetic appreciation, moral evaluation, and religious faith in terms of what it means for us to look. A great work of art, he suggests, demands that we look and look and look—and then be prepared to look again. We can return to a painting we have known for years and discover something new or reread a novel and find an insight that we missed the first time that seemed intended especially for us. Art has these depths that call us to constantly look again. Williams suggests that such looking again is also morally necessary. What hideous damage has been done, after all, when a definitive judgment is made about a person or community and the judges never bother to look again. As a great painting demands I look again, so all human beings, especially those I may be inclined to deal with quickly, require repeated looking to begin to appreciate who is before us and how we can respond adequately.[74] Finally, Williams ties these aesthetic and moral "seeings" to religious seeing, in which the believer has faith in "a perspective that we can only speak of as representing unrestricted time, total self-investment ... for the Christian (or Jew or Muslim) it is the perspective of an active creator."[75] The completeness of God's seeing for Williams, then, refers not only to faith in God's omniscience; it also refers to God's capacity to see creatures in their fullness, as God's seeing is not compromised by a grasping or insecure ego.

To bring yourself alone before God, then, may be a means of attending to how God sees you. Of course, the influence that belief

---

[74]Rowan Williams, "Has Secularism Failed?" in *Faith in the Public Square* (New York: Bloomsbury, 2012), 13–14.
[75]Ibid., 18.

in God's seeing has will depend on what sort of God one has faith in. Such a belief may—and indeed has been—used in illegitimate ways and to destructive purposes. An ever-present God who is the omniscient equivalent of a nagging parent, an angry boss, or a needy friend, among other possibilities, is not the kind of companion any of us need. I am reminded that on the door of a church near where I live, there is a sticker that reads, "God is watching, and so are we: premises under twenty-four hour surveillance." The analogy between God's seeing and surveillance cameras conveys that both are at the ready if you do anything naughty. I understand that for Jesus, and for Augustine, while God's seeing of us is certainly true, and therefore notices our faults, it is also marked by unbounded love for us. A practice of self-criticism founded in belief in such a God, then, will regard oneself and others as beloved creatures of God. As we shall see, to attend to God's seeing in solitude, then, may involve pursuing a more exacting self-criticism, as belief in God's complete seeing of me may apply a certain pressure to be more honest with myself. I may as well acknowledge before God what God already knows better than I do. As well, God's seeing is believed to be a loving seeing, and so it may also open me up to see the goodness in myself that dwelling exclusively on my faults may tend to eclipse. Augustine develops this line of thinking, discussed in the next chapter, in relation to his conception of conscience. Another influence that belief in God's seeing may play is when I examine my relationships with others, I may criticize my own seeing of them in the light of how God sees them. Augustine's in-depth consideration of this sort of self-interrogation will be the subject of the third chapter. In all these ways, solitude in God's company may support me to look again and look better because of the influence of considering God's own looking. Solitude, of course, is not the only place to do such looking, but it is the argument of this book that it may be one, especially effective, place to do so. In the next chapter, as we turn to Augustine, we shall see how he interpreted Jesus's teaching on solitude that we considered in this chapter.

2

The Privacy of Conscience

Beware of practicing your piety before others in order
to be seen by them; for then you have no reward from your
Father in heaven ... But whenever you pray, go into your
room and shut the door and pray to your Father who is in
secret; and your Father who sees in secret will reward you.

—MATTHEW 6:1, 6

We begin our consideration of Augustine with his interpretation of Jesus's teaching on solitude in the Sermon on the Mount, which we considered in the last chapter. One of Augustine's first biblical commentaries focused on these chapters of the Gospel of Matthew. After he was ordained a priest, he wrote to his bishop asking for some time to study the Bible. He had studied the Bible before, but as a new priest he no doubt felt considerable professional pressure to increase his Scriptural knowledge—and quickly. Prior to his ordination, he had written a commentary on Genesis, and he would begin another commentary on it soon after he was ordained. The first New Testament commentary he wrote was on the Sermon on the Mount. He was innovating in his choice to separate out these chapters from the rest of the Gospel of Matthew.[1] In so doing, he inaugurated a tradition of considering this section as a concise and coherent summary of Jesus's moral teaching. Augustine's choice to write his first New Testament

---

[1]Boniface Ramsey, "Introduction," in *The Lord's Sermon on the Mount*, ed. Augustine, *The New Testament I and II* (New York: New City Press, 2014), 11.

commentary on the Sermon on the Mount indicates the priority he placed on it. This early commentary will serve as an introduction to Augustine's thinking on solitude. While Augustine would never return to write another commentary on the Sermon on the Mount, these verses remained firmly in his mind, as he regularly refers to them throughout his career in other works, which we will also draw on. In particular, we shall see how the contrast between acting for others' approval (their seeing) and God's approval (God's seeing) is central to his masterpiece of cultural analysis, *The City of God*.

Augustine interprets Jesus's teaching on solitude in terms of a distinction between "outer" and "inner" parts of the human being, and the "inner" includes our "conscience." Augustine believes that true solitude involves turning "within" and bringing oneself alone before God; even if we may have achieved an external solitude, in that we are away from other human companions, we may not have come to an internal solitude, in which we dwell in God's company. For Augustine, we all have a built-in space for solitude, as we can withdraw into our consciences and there be alone with God. This space is especially set apart for self-examination. He argues that a Christian practice of solitude in this inner space makes a number of consequential differences to one's life, as we shall see.

Augustine's interpretation of Jesus's teaching on solitude

Augustine thinks self-examination alone before God is one way to confront what I will refer to as performative goodness, which he believes Jesus criticizes. Augustine often frames his discussion of solitude in terms of an apparent contradiction in Jesus's teaching on the Sermon on the Mount between verses that command maximum publicity (" ... let your light shine before others, so that they may see your good works"[2]) and privacy ("Beware of practicing your piety before others in order to be seen by them ... "[3]).[4] Jesus is

---

[2]Mt. 5:16.
[3]Mt. 6:1.
[4]See, for example, *Sermons*, 54.3 and 338.3; *City of God*, 5.14; *Homilies on the First Epistle of John*, 6.3.

not, Augustine says, contradicting himself or giving "contrary orders."[5] The command to seek solitude is directed toward those who do good as a performance and "make such a song and dance of their good works because they see the whole point of their good works to be praise from people."[6] They seek recognition for being good themselves, "parading their glory" in public so that they can convince others of their "indispensability."[7] This performative goodness is, in Augustine's view, the very definition of the hypocrisy that Jesus condemns. To act primarily for others' eyes is to play a part. "Hypocrites are impersonators, mouthpieces for their characters, as in stories from the theatre," he writes in his first commentary, "[a hypocrite] impersonates a [just] man but does not exhibit his qualities, because he derives all his satisfaction from the praise of people, which impersonators can also do."[8] When performing, one's action does not flow from one's character or from a desire to do another good; instead, every action is calibrated to earn applause from a favored audience. Augustine indicates here that performative goodness, even if it can persuade others for a while that it is genuine, will finally prove wanting; the actor's make-up will begin to crack eventually.

Yet Augustine does not take Jesus to be suggesting that the alternative to performative goodness is privacy or anonymity. Jesus is instructing his followers instead to do good in public in order to burnish God's reputation, not theirs: "[their works] should be pleasing to human beings so that [in those works] God may be glorified."[9] Augustine thinks that this reorients what it means to do good; the self is not at the center but acts as a medium by which the goodness that is received from God is then relayed to others. Jesus's metaphor of putting a lamp on a stand rather than under a bushel[10] is an image of how Jesus's followers should be seen to

---

[5]Augustine, *Expositions of the Psalms (51–72)*, trans. Maria Boulding (New York: New City Press, 2001), 65.3.
[6]Augustine, *Sermons (20–50)*, trans. Edmund Hill (New York: New City Press, 1990), 47.13.
[7]Ibid., 54.2.
[8]Augustine, *The Lord's Sermon on the Mount*, trans. Michael G. Campbell, in *The New Testament I and II*, 2.2.5.
[9]Ibid., 1.7.18.
[10]Mt. 5:15.

reflect God's goodness, so that their example inspires and instructs others.[11] This kind of publicity has a different relation to goodness because the follower of Jesus recognizes herself as a recipient of whatever goodness she is capable of; and, as a recipient, she has a responsibility to make goodness available to others too and not take primary credit for it. Acting publicly, then, is an act of "generosity."[12]

Augustine divides the benefit of a good work that others can see in two; there is a "material" and "spiritual" good. The material good is the need that is met, like feeding someone, whereas the spiritual good is the example that is made public for others' encouragement and imitation. Augustine is especially adamant about how we need exemplars of generous goodness: "If you are afraid that people will see you, you will have no imitators; therefore you should be seen. But that isn't why you should allow yourself to be seen."[13] The witnesses of such good works will not only delight in God who acts in those others; witnessing those works will also give them hope that they too are capable of such admirable deeds.[14] Goodness is not possessed and performed but received and passed on. Publicity is an essential means of that passing on.

Whereas we characterized acting primarily for others' approval as performative goodness, we shall denote the opposite as communicative goodness. This adjective has a long history, going back to the New Testament. While generally we use "communication" only to refer to the sharing of information, the larger sense of the term, as O'Donovan writes, "is to hold something as common, to make it a common possession, to treat it as 'ours', rather than 'yours' or 'mine'. The partners to a communication form a community, a 'we,' in relation to the object in which they participate."[15] Augustine regards the primary purpose of human action as communicating the ultimate public good, the goodness of God; it is a public good because it is meant to be shared universally, and it is not lessened

---

[11]Augustine, *The Lord's Sermon on the Mount*, 1.6.17.

[12]Ibid., 1.7.19.

[13]*Homilies on the First Epistle of John*, trans. Boniface Ramsey (New York: New City Press, 2008), 6.3.

[14]*Sermons*, 54.2.

[15]Oliver O'Donovan, *Ways of Judgment* (Grand Rapids, MI: Eerdmans, 2005), 242.

by being shared. There remains here a profound affirmation of individuality, because your sharing of God's goodness distinctively reflects *you*. Thus Augustine interprets Jesus as recommending public action so that God's goodness may be communicated, but not for the sake of one's own reputation; whatever good one receives from God is meant to be held in common, to form a public that is, or becomes, a "we." By contrast, as we shall consider further below, performative goodness seeks others' approval that becomes "mine" by securing a positive perception of me or my tribe.

Solitude before God is one way to wean oneself off of the desire for others' approval, which defines performative goodness. Augustine maps Jesus's distinction between seeking others' approval and God's onto an anthropological distinction between inner and outer. When puzzling over Jesus's saying that when giving charitably, you should not let your left hand know what your right hand is doing, Augustine interprets the right hand as acting "interiorly in secret" for an "inner reward," whereas the left hand represents "everything external that is visible and temporal," which are all forms of an "outer reward."[16] Augustine also specifies that this "inner reward" is "within a good conscience": "What does *in secret* mean if not within a good conscience that cannot be shown to the human eye nor disclosed in words? ... [I]f you are looking for a reward from the one who alone scrutinizes the conscience, let conscience itself suffice to merit your reward."[17] To act primarily to be seen by God in secret is to pursue the inner reward within conscience.

Augustine assumes that we depend on recognition, the question is whether we seek that recognition primarily from others or from God. In a sermon, for example, after having repeated that Christians ought not to act in order to receive others' praise, he quips, "Now, now, don't get angry because [God] is glorified; stay with God and you will be glorified with God." How are we somehow glorified "with God"? Augustine's answer: "The testimony of our conscience is our glory and boast, because it is in God."[18] Thus the conscience, which is characterized as inner, has its own "testimony," its own means of approval and disapproval, and thereby it mediates God's

---

[16]Augustine, *The Lord's Sermon on the Mount*, 2.2.9.
[17]Ibid.
[18]*Sermons (20–50)*, 47.13.

reward within. As he elaborates elsewhere, "Let your conscience bear testimony to you, because it is from God ... Let him who crowns see it; let him be your witness by whom, as your judge, you are crowned."[19] It may be, then, that one receives no outer approval in terms of others' approval, but God's approval is plentiful within: "Your outer storeroom is empty, your inner coffers are full. Full coffers are a good conscience."[20] Augustine teaches the way to wean ourselves off of other's approval is to turn inward to examine the testimony of our conscience alone before God.

Augustine represents the inner as having a spaciousness to it. We have this built-in space for solitude that is always at the ready; while taking some time for introspection generally requires getting away from people for awhile, Augustine also depicts it as occurring inside a roomy chamber that belongs to each of us. In commenting on Jesus's instruction to pray in one's "room" he takes it as our hearts: "our bedroom is our heart."[21] We can withdraw into ourselves— "the inner recesses of our heart"—and there shut the door from "all the temporal and visible things that enter our thoughts by the door of the fleshly senses and disturb them through a multitude of futile images." We are to resist these images so that we may utter a "spiritual prayer ... where we pray to the Father in secret, may be directed to the Father."[22] Augustine refers to this inward prayer as a kind of dialogue with God in which we are "either asking that something be done for [us] or consulting [God] about what [we] should do."[23] There are, then, levels to this interiority, as we can plunge further and further until we stand alone before God where God alone sees. True solitude, for Augustine, demands that we enter this inner space and bring ourselves intentionally before God.

We have seen this kind of dialogue with and before God earlier, in the Psalms and in Jesus's life, most prominently in the Garden of Gethsemane. Augustine locates it as occurring in this inner space that is always already there within us, awaiting us to enter

---

[19]*Homilies on the First Epistle of John*, 6.3.
[20]*Sermons (20–50)*, 25A.2.3.
[21]*Expositions of the Psalms (33–50)*, trans. Maria Boulding (New York: New City Press, 2000), 35.5.
[22]Augustine, *The Lord's Sermon on the Mount*, 2.3.11.
[23]*Letters (100–155)*, trans. Roland Teske (New York: New City Press, 2003), 140.29.69.

it. The possibility of entering into dialogue with God, and doing so as a means to temporarily withdraw from others, is inherent to our humanity. This all takes place where others cannot see or hear: "Where heard the Lord? Within. Where gives He? Within. There you pray, there you are heard, there you are blessed ... and he knows not who stands by you: it is all carried on in secret."[24] Thus this inner space is the ideal place in which to evaluate the effect others' approval has on us and instead deliberate about what would most gain God's approval: "No man or woman sees what you are thinking, but God sees it. Take care, then, to pour out your prayer where no one sees except the one who rewards you."[25] But we are not telling God something God doesn't already know; instead to speak with God in this way is a reflection of our creaturely dependence on God. We are seeking God's goodness, which does not originate with us, but must be communicated to us by God because a "rational creature ... is not for itself the good by which it comes blessed; but that good is immutable by participating in which the rational creature is also made wise."[26] Dialogue with and before God in this inner space is a crucial means of participating in God's abundant goodness.

Distinguishing between "inner" and "outer"

To explore further the significance of Augustine's distinction between inner and outer, we must trace out what is implied with this metaphor and also some of the key sources of Augustine's depiction of it. Doing so will help us to better understand the particular contours of Augustine's understanding of solitude. To begin, the most basic origin of any distinction between inner and outer is a fact of our anatomy, as Denys Turner convincingly argues. When I consider my (or another's) thinking or feeling, I do not have

---

[24]*Expositions of the Psalms (33–50)*, 35.5.
[25]*Expositions of the Psalms (121–150)*, trans. Maria Boulding (New York: New City Press, 2004), 141.3.
[26]*Letters (100–155)*, 140.29.69.

a visible feature of anatomy to focus on; the brain and heart lie under the surface of our skin (most of the time, thankfully) and so outside my observation and therefore may be called "inner." By contrast, if I consider other parts of anatomy, like hair, I do have a visible feature to focus on (or not, as in my case) and so this may be called "outer."[27] This "physical fact" of our make-up means that such a distinction between "inner" and "outer" is a commonplace, frequently buried in words we regularly use. Since the Introduction we have been bumping into one key example: "introspection," which literally means "looking inside." How we represent and interpret the significance of this anatomical fact is another question.

One formative influence on Augustine is the biblical representation of the heart. For the biblical tradition the heart is identified as the source of thinking and feeling.[28] We saw in the previous chapter that the psalmist refers to the heart in such a way that implies dialogue with oneself before God, as in Psalm 77: "To my own heart I speak, and my spirit inquires"[29] and Psalm 4: "Quake and do not offend. / Speak in your hearts and on your beds, and be still."[30] So too in First Samuel, for example, when Hannah "was speaking in her heart" in prayer before God, her lips were moving but she was not speaking audibly, so Eli thought she was drunk.[31] As in the latter case, descriptions of the heart may picture it as having a certain depth to it, that is, it is turned away from the observer. In other words, what I can observe from your words and actions may not necessarily conform to what is going on in your heart. Jesus speaks about the heart in this way. In the Sermon on the Mount, for example, he says that even if you commit adultery in your heart, and don't commit it in the world, it is still a sin.[32] Even so, the depth of the heart is never pictured in the biblical tradition, to my knowledge, as something we can *enter*. The heart is described as a kind of container, but not as having enough room that you can

---

[27]Turner, *The Darkness of God: Negativity in Christian Mysticism* (Cambridge: Cambridge University Press, 1998), 91.

[28]See, for example, Deut. 15: 10 and 28:47; 1 Kgs 3:12 and 8:38.

[29]Ps. 77:7, trans. Alter.

[30]Ps. 4:5, trans. Alter.

[31]See also Deut. 8:17, 9:4, 18:21.

[32]Mt. 5:28. For other references to heart in Matthew, see 9:4 and 15:19. In the latter verse, Jesus makes clear that what is in the heart cannot remain indefinitely hidden.

go inside it. So we must also look elsewhere to make sense of the remarkable spaciousness that Augustine attributes to our "interior."

Another primary influence, outside the biblical tradition, is the third-century Platonic philosopher Plotinus. It is thanks, in part,[33] to Plotinus's influence that Augustine will depict the inner as having enough space that we can enter and dwell there in solitude. Augustine frequently distinguishes between inner and outer when he is addressing how we make judgments, and his understanding of this process is decidedly shaped by Plotinus. The activity of judgment for Augustine is a key to what is distinctive about us as creatures made in God's image. While Augustine's understanding of judgment includes the narrow sense that may initially spring to our minds—as when we decide whether something someone says is false—he also has a much broader sense of what judging involves. Judgment includes all the interpretive acts that we are constantly engaged in as creatures who think and love. To be capable of such interpretive acts means that we are not passively determined by our experience, but can actively engage with it through, among other means, making evaluations and telling stories. We have already been considering judgments in this chapter, because seeking others' approval is a means by which we decide how to act. It is not surprising, then, that the language of "inner" and "outer" appears when Augustine is commenting on Jesus's moral teaching.

The inner spaciousness comes from Plotinus's belief that we have access within us to the ideas that orient true judgments. These ideas comprise the first level of what J. P. Kenney refers to as Plotinus's "double transcendence theory"; "double" denotes two levels of transcendence, both of which are divine.[34] We will now consider how Augustine appropriates the first level, the ideas that orient true judgments, and will later return in the conclusion of this chapter to how he rejects the second level, Plotinus's radical conception of the highest divine principle, the One. Augustine's complex negotiation with Plotinus's theology distinctly informs his understanding of solitude.

---

[33]I take Plotinus to be a major influence on Augustine's understanding of inner space and so my focus will be on him. Phillip Cary also argues persuasively for other ancient influences on Augustine, including ancient representations of human memory as an "inner world" and Cicero's descriptions of the soul; see Phillip Cary, *Augustine's Invention of the Inner Self* (Oxford: Oxford University Press, 2000), 125–139.

[34]J. P. Kenney, *Contemplation and Classical Christianity* (Oxford: Oxford University Press, 2013), 16.

Plotinus's first level of transcendence exists immaterially and transcends the material universe, yet is the basis for all that exists; every physical thing derives its existence and nature from immaterial ideas or forms that exist in the "intelligible" level of transcendence. Some who held to this view understood the divine to be a Mind that unceasingly thinks these ideas. For Plotinus, we are able to make true judgments of things because a part of our soul remains in constant union with that divine Mind, and therefore we have access to those ideas. In his treatise *On Beauty*, Plotinus argues that when we find something beautiful, we do so because of how the beautiful material thing dimly reflects the source of its being, its immaterial idea. Beautiful things, then, he writes, are nothing but "images and traces and shadows." Rather than looking at the outward shadow, we must turn within to the see the real thing. We can only do so after a long process of spiritual transformation; eventually, we may turn within to see "the intelligible world," which contains "all the beautiful Forms" and learn that "these Ideas are what Beauty is."[35] As we turn from what is without to what is within, we discover these ideas within our soul; these ideas are always available for us to see them, if we have the ability to do so.

Even with this brief description, Plotinus implies a sense of spaciousness to the inner. The inner has a content to it; indeed, the inner is jam-packed because it contains the ideas of all things. Phillip Cary insightfully notes that the very way Plotinus frames this movement from outer to inner lays the ground for a metaphor of inner space, because in turning away from the outer world we turn toward an inner one. The momentum of the metaphor, we might say, inevitably leads to attributing space to our interiority. Not only that, Cary further observes, the inner world has something inside it that we can look at, so there also needs to be enough space to turn around.[36]

Augustine takes on Plotinus's distinction between inner and outer when analyzing how we make judgments.[37] Many of our judgments

---

[35]Plotinus, *The Enneads*, trans. George Boys-Stones, ed. Lloyd P. Gerson (Cambridge: Cambridge University Press, 2018), 1.6.8–1.6.9.

[36]Cary, *Augustine's Invention of the Inner Self*, 63–64.

[37]For key examples of Augustine's descriptions of how we make judgments, see *On Free Will*, 2.3.7–2.15.39; *Confessions*, 7.10.16, 7.17.23, 10.7.11; *True Religion*, 29.52–31.38.

happen so quickly—about whether something is right or wrong, or beautiful or ugly—that we are likely only partially conscious of what they involve. The distinction between inner and outer is necessary to trace out one of the crucial turns involved in making a judgment. We generally make our judgments about something or someone that we encounter in the world; Augustine refers to this object of our judgment as "outer." In order to discern the basis of our judgment, though, we must turn to what is "inner," namely the intellectual acts that were involved in coming to whatever judgment we've made. And then, there is a final turn, as we move from what is "inner" to what is "upper," when we discover, as Augustine thinks we will if we are capable of it, that the intellectual acts in which we make a judgment are dependent on a standard against which that judgment is made and, ultimately, that standard itself is dependent on God's constant presence to our minds. Augustine's adoption of Plotinus's understanding of judgment, then, includes the "inner" as having enough space for us not only to enter but also to look up.

As well, the three moments involved in a judgment (outward, inward, and upward) are also steps in a hierarchy that we climb as we move from what is mutable and dependent to what is immutable and independent. In *Confessions*, Augustine tells of how it was reading "books of the Platonists"[38] that finally enabled him to recognize the existence of immaterial realities; his inability to affirm the existence of immaterial realities was preventing him from taking Christianity seriously, given that its understanding of human beings and of God depends on there being more than matter in motion. When he followed Plotinus's advice and turned within, he saw the activity of his own mind, an immaterial activity; and, further, he also discovered the presence of God to his mind, another immaterial activity, as the very foundation of his thinking.[39]

The influence of Plotinus's first level of transcendence is evident from Augustine's understanding of judgment; adopting this understanding

---

[38]*Confessions*, 7.9.13.
[39]*Confessions*, 7.10.16–7.17.23. This is not so say that reference to God as standard is directly involved for all of our judgments. Augustine does think, though, that in tracing why we make the judgments that we do, eventually we will come to the desire for happiness; and the desire for happiness for him, however differently we may pursue it, is ultimately a form of the desire for God. And so, the ultimate standard of our judgments, we might say, is God; see *Confessions*, 10.20.29–10.23.33.

of judgment means that Augustine takes on the metaphor of inner space that, as we have already seen, he uses to interpret Jesus's teaching on solitude. Yet he also departs from Plotinus's interpretation of this first level, which makes a distinct difference to how Augustine represents that inner space. Augustine's inner space is more properly private, open to God alone, and this will be key to the difference that a practice of solitude may make. This increased sense of privacy that belongs to Augustine's inner space comes from how he distinguishes between the divine and the human. As we saw in the passage from Plotinus's *On Beauty*, there was no firm distinction between turning inward to our soul and then entering the divine Mind where we encounter the ideas. There are only, as Cary puts it, two steps: from outer to inner; once we've turned within, the ideas are there to see.[40] While doing so will require moral and intellectual discipline, eventually we can turn within to gaze upon the divine Mind. This is possible because, for Plotinus, the highest part of our souls is divine. What is most essential for us in all of this is that, for Plotinus, we all have access to that mind of God, so that inner space is finally a public space. We may all gaze on the ideas that underlie all things; what most defines your "interior" is also what most defines my "interior."

Cary argues, rightly in my view, that Augustine ultimately could not accept the view that the highest part of our selves is constantly united to the mind of God. He outlines the result of Augustine's disagreement with Plotinus on this point:

> [For Plotinus] in turning "into the inside", toward the highest and truest and best part of itself, the soul is turning to the world of divine Mind, which is not private property but common to all souls who contemplate it. The mature Augustine cannot follow him here. Once Augustine fully understands the Nicene [Creed's] Creator/creature distinction, he can no longer consider the best part of the soul to be divine or immutable. The soul has its own kind of being, distinct from the immutable being of God above and from the spatial being of bodies below it, and hence it belongs at a middle level on the ontological hierarchy, beneath the intelligible world and above the sensible world.[41]

---

[40]Cary, *Augustine's Invention of the Inner Self*, 117.
[41]Ibid., 116.

When Augustine makes this cut, Cary concludes, we have a "new concept of inner privacy."[42] This comes from the fact that, for Augustine, there is not a seamless transition from going inward to accessing the ideas, the first level of transcendence. Augustine would certainly agree with Plotinus that if our judgment is true, it does not belong to us, because truth is public. Yet Augustine's inner space is distinct from those ideas; thus it is a place of the utmost privacy, where God alone can see us—a place perfectly suited for obeying Jesus's instruction that we are to pray, fast, and give alms before "your Father, who sees in secret."[43]

Augustine on conscience

To now see better the moral value of this private, inner space, we need to consider Augustine's conception of conscience.[44] For Augustine conscience refers to both a place—our private inner space—and an activity, namely self-criticism before God. Ian Clausen puts this point well: "To occupy the place of conscience is to re-possess moral self-consciousness ... conscience rings synonymous with agency, responsibility, basically anything that lifts humanity into the realm of the moral life."[45] Before we turn to examine Augustine's conception of conscience further, we ought to briefly indicate some sense of the history of the idea. We do not have the space, or the need, to delve deeply into the etymological and theoretical complexities of this history. Richard Sorabji offers us a brief sketch of conscience prior to Augustine that gives an overview that will suffice for our purposes:

> The idea of conscience started in ancient Greek thought as the idea of awareness of one's own fault or weakness, then of one's

---

[42]Ibid.

[43]Mt. 6:4.

[44]I note that despite Cary's extensive treatment of Augustine's "inner space," Cary does not discuss conscience. I suspect if he added such a discussion, it would problematize some of the moral grounds on which he condemns Augustine's account of interiority.

[45]Ian Clausen, "Seeking the Place of Conscience in Higher Education: An Augustinian View," *Religions*, no. 6 (2015): 288.

own faultlessness and even, especially in Roman texts, of one's own merit. The expression used for conscience also covered the idea of awareness of the fault, faultlessness, or merit. Although there was an idea of right or wrong in general, and indeed of a natural law of right or wrong, it was not directly connected with expressions of conscience. Saint Paul was innovating, then, when he connected an expression for conscience closely with the idea of a general *law* of right and wrong.[46]

We can see already here the connection between Augustine's interest in judgment and the history of conscience. Conscience involves one's judgments of oneself, most frequently of one's wrongdoing, occasionally of the opposite. Sorabji also helpfully notes the metaphor implicitly at work with conscience, as every individual is represented as though "composed of two people. One of them knows of the defect but is keeping it a secret; the other shares the secret—in cases of moral conscience, a guilty one."[47] Sorabji also identifies an undoubted influence on Augustine's thinking on conscience with the "innovation" of Paul.

We may now turn to Augustine with some sense of conscience's history in view. Before explicitly connecting Augustine's sense of conscience with the practice of solitude, a survey of his use of the term will serve as a foundation.[48] One challenge in making sense of Augustine on conscience is that Latin does not distinguish "consciousness" and "conscience," as English does. He can use the term, then, simply to indicate the direction of our attention[49] or what we have in mind when acting.[50] In its adjectival form it corresponds to this more general sense of being "conscious" or "aware" of something.[51] This general sense of consciousness does include a sense of privacy because my consciousness is known partly

---

[46]Richard Sorabji, "Graeco-Roman Origins of the Idea of Moral Conscience," *Studia Patristica*, no. 44 (2010): 362.

[47]Richard Sorabji, *Moral Conscience through the Ages: Fifth Century BCE to the Present* (Chicago: University of Chicago Press, 2014), 12.

[48]This analysis is based on a word search for all the mentions of conscience in Augustine's sermons and letters.

[49]*Sermons*, 60A.4.

[50]*Sermons*, 149.12.

[51]See *Sermons*, 293.12 and *Letters*, 23.1.

by me and only fully by God.[52] In communication with one another this privacy of our consciousness presents a constant challenge. As, for example, when another thinks I am lying, I have no way of demonstrating that what I am saying is indeed what I think, because I cannot "open" to him my "inner thoughts where God alone is witness."[53] Thus, true intimacy would involve knowing not just another's body but his consciousness.[54]

As opposed to this more general meaning of "conscientia" as "consciousness," there is the more specific sense that is similar to our "conscience." We are reserving the latter term for our *moral* self-consciousness—that is, when consciousness is engaged specifically in approval or disapproval of our actions, thoughts, and feelings. The relation is surely not difficult to discern, for my evaluations ("conscience") are an object and activity of my awareness ("consciousness"). Thus, "conscience" is a result of how human beings are constantly making judgments with their "consciousnesses." Those judgments include the moral ones we make about ourselves. As with the ancient tradition reviewed above, Augustine often refers to conscience in relation to an uncomfortable sense that we may have that we did wrong: the person who does wrong "suffers the torments of his conscience in the inner chamber of his heart."[55]

How does Augustine describe this pain? The most common description is of our conscience being "pricked" or of itself "pricking."[56] This verb describes the sense of wrongdoing as a frequent nuisance. This corresponds nicely with an image Augustine uses to describe a guilty conscience: that of a nagging spouse.[57] In more severe cases, Augustine describes our conscience as "tormented,"[58] "wounded,"[59] and "bloodstained."[60] These other descriptors no longer present the conscience as a nagging spouse;

---

[52]*Sermons*, 12.3, 14.4 and 30.3; *Letters*, 144.5 and 153.19.
[53]*Sermons (1–19)*, trans. Edmund Hill (New York: New City Press, 1990), 12.3.
[54]*Sermons*, 267.1
[55]*Sermons (145–183)*, trans. Edmund Hill (New York: New City Press, 1992), 180.7.8.
[56]*Sermons*, 37.10, 89.1, 99.3, 208.2, and 350.3.
[57]*Expositions of the Psalms*, second exposition of *Psalm*, 33.8.
[58]*Sermons*, 180.8.
[59]Ibid., 82.11.
[60]Ibid.

instead, the better image is that of an enemy within.[61] Yet both images indicate the result of a guilty conscience: a sense of oneself as divided and of a conflict within; our moral self-consciousness is pulled two ways, as it cannot fully attend to what is immediately present to it, but it is also dominated by the awareness of some wrongdoing. The result is that our roomy inner space becomes positively claustrophobic.

The most common adjective used to describe the opposite of a guilty conscience is simply a "good" one.[62] Whereas awareness of wrongdoing "pricks" and "torments" us, Augustine frequently describes how a "good" conscience is "calm"[63] and "clear"[64] allowing us to get some sleep! Unlike a bad conscience, which is wounded and bloody, a good one is "clean"[65] and "healthy."[66] Such a conscience, as we have already seen, is a roomy, inner space, like a bedroom,[67] a desert retreat,[68] or comfortable home.[69] Whereas a bad conscience is described as a nagging wife or aggressive enemy, indicating a lack of space within, a good conscience is peaceful and roomy—a built-in place of solitude.

How do we put together conscience as moral self-consciousness with conscience as an inner space? The place of conscience supports the work of self-examination in solitude before God. Augustine's depiction of interiority, then, attributes to conscience a kind of privacy that makes it perfectly equipped to deliberate on what I should do and reflect on what I have done. This interior privacy, as we saw above in Augustine's comments on Jesus's Sermon on the Mount, is put to use in a Christian practice of solitude. The Christian may withdraw into the solitude of her conscience in order to consider what would receive God's approval (the "interior reward") and how that relates to what might earn others' approval

---

[61]*Letters*, 73.10.
[62]See, for example, *Sermons*, 12.3, 37.10, 47.11, 107.7.8, and 137.11.14.
[63]Ibid., 38.8.
[64]Ibid., 306.10.
[65]Ibid., 47.8.
[66]Ibid., 133.4.
[67]Augustine, *The Lord's Sermon on the Mount*, 2.3.11; and *Expositions of the Psalms*, 35.5.
[68]*Expositions of the Psalms*, 54.9; and *Sermons*, 47.23.
[69]*Expositions of the Psalms*, second exposition of Psalms 33.8 and 100.4.

(the "exterior reward"). Doing so, as we will consider in the next section, has decisive implications for one's practice of self-criticism.[70]

A literary image of conscience may serve to draw together our analysis of Augustine's understanding of conscience thus far. In Jane Austen's *Mansfield Park*, our heroine, Fanny Price, leaves her impoverished family to live with her wealthy uncle. As is typical in Austen's marvelous novels, *Mansfield Park* charts the coming-of-age of an intelligent woman who is faced with navigating moral dilemmas that are bound up with the vexing question of whom to marry. There are many advantages to Fanny's new life at her rich uncle's home (and not a few disadvantages too); the advantage that most concerns us is the spacious room that she claims as her own, which, in my reading, is an image of conscience. While the bedroom she was given and continues to use is a tiny attic, she gradually spends more and more time in the abandoned schoolroom, until others regard it as hers, not having any use for it themselves. This process itself indicates how her "East room" is acknowledged as her private space within the

---

[70]My focus on conscience offers a fresh way to approach scholarly debates about the nature and legacy of "Augustinian interiority." Some influential scholars have, in my view, fallen into the trap of presenting the relation between inner and outer in Augustine in terms of two extremes: either they are distinguished sharply from one another or any difference between them is collapsed. Authors who take the former approach include Charles Taylor and Phillip Cary; see Taylor, *Sources of the Self* (Boston: Harvard University Press, 1992), 129–135, and Cary, *Augustine's Invention of the Inner Self*, vii–xvi. Authors who take the latter approach include Charles Mathewes and Michael Hanby; see Mathewes, *A Theology of Public Life* (Cambridge: Cambridge University Press, 2008), 47–56, and Hanby, *Augustine and Modernity* (New York: Routledge, 2003), 35–47. As I show in the remainder of this chapter and the subsequent one, when explored in relation to Augustine's understanding of conscience, inner and outer are integrally related for the Christian. Augustine does describe, as we have seen, an "inner space" where we can dwell alone before God. Therefore, any attempt to elide the difference between "inner" and "outer" does not reflect the priority the inner space of conscience plays for Augustine. And yet those solitary "inner" moments before God support us to turn "outward" again to love others better. So simply distinguishing "inner" and "outer" from one another, which traces out the dynamic relation between them, doesn't reflect the subtlety of Augustine's thinking either. Not to mention that, as we shall see, Augustine encourages the Christian to hope for the day when the distinction between inner and outer is overcome, when in heaven all will enjoy perfect communion with one another and God.

house. Compared to her attic bed-room, the narrator tells us the "East room" is "more spacious and more meet for walking about in, and thinking, and of which she had now from some time been almost equally mistress." That she was "mistress" of this room indicates how it belongs to her and she has responsibility for it. As well, we are given an example of the kind of walking she does in it, as when she is facing a difficult decision about "what she *ought to do*" she walks around her room and engages in dialogue with herself: "Was she *right* in refusing what was so warmly asked, so strongly wished for? ... Was it not ill-nature—selfishness, and a fear of exposing herself?"[71] The walking that can take place in this spacious room, then, is an embodied form of intense self-examination and self-criticism.

This dialogue takes place in a room that is suffused with the influences and authorities that inform Fanny's deliberation, which depicts all that belongs to her conscience. As we will see with Augustine too, conscience includes a range of influences and authorities that the individual engages with. It is surely not an accident, for example, that Fanny's room was previously the schoolroom, in which she and her cousins received their education. And Fanny has now furnished it with her books and plants, which represent how her conscience is informed by the thoughts of others and her study of nature; and her room is decorated with gifts given by family and friends, which indicates the role that memory plays in her deliberations. We are told of how she engaged in active recollection in which she considered and reconsidered the bad done to her, but also found a way to console herself when mistreated and to reconcile herself to others. Thus we are informed of Fanny's practice of forgiving others. As well, the art on the walls includes depictions of her family, as well as Tintern Abbey, a cave in Italy, and a moonlight lake in Cumberland. Several of these images subtly reflect the image of the literary movement of Romanticism on Fanny.[72] As with the case of the plants, two of these three prints indicate Fanny's love for nature. Elsewhere in the novel, Fanny speaks at length about the positive

---

[71]Jane Austen, *Mansfield Park* (1814; New York: Penguin Books, 1996), 141.
[72]I am grateful to my colleague Margaret Kirby for alerting me to this connection with Romanticism.

role nature can play in one's moral formation as it draws you out of yourself to a larger sense of things.[73]

Fanny's conscience, then, is a private space that embodies all of the influences and authorities that she takes into account when she is engaged in deliberation and self-criticism. While there is something decidedly private about her room, it also reflects an openness to learning from a variety of sources. I do not want to spoil the twists and turns of this arresting novel; suffice it to say that Fanny's ability to withstand others' attempts to influence a major decision she has to make is due, at least in part, to the time she spends alone in the solitude of her conscience. Certainly Augustine and Fanny would not entirely agree on the influences and authorities that ought to be involved in one's self-criticism. Even so, Augustine's sense of conscience, like Fanny's "East Room," brings together a process of self-interrogation with a location, a private space where one can retreat from the influence of others.

Conscience in Augustine and Austen may seem foreign to some of the contemporary senses of the term, if we are used to thinking of conscience as a trustworthy inner voice or an angel on our shoulder. O'Donovan captures well the contrast between conscience as we have it here and some of its later developments that are alive today. Above all, he stresses, conscience in Christian tradition is a "consistently *discursive* self-consciousness, a roomy mental space for reflection and deliberation." He continues:

> Conscience was memory in responsibility, the workshop of practical reason, a formal rather than an efficient or final cause. Insofar as it laid claim to authority, it was simply the believer's authority to reach decisions reflectively rather than accept decisions made for him by others … But the sovereignty of conscience [in later thinking] imported a kind of peremptory immediacy, cutting short deliberation and negotiation … And with this it changed from a guarantee of freedom into a tyrant. The rational agent was left helpless before the voice that came from nowhere and could by mediated by no rational argument.[74]

---

[73]Ibid., 105–106. I am grateful to my colleague Margaret Kirby for calling into question whether Fanny, in fact, ever has a direct encounter with nature, and contrasting Fanny with Elizabeth Bennett, the heroine of *Pride and Prejudice*, who most certainly does.
[74]O'Donovan, *Ways of Judgment*, 302.

Having gained some clarity on Augustine's conception of conscience, we can now turn to see what difference such a practice of solitude makes.

The difference conscience makes

To identify the difference a Christian practice of solitude can make, we turn to contrasts Augustine makes between those who seek inner reward within conscience and those who seek the outer reward of others' approval. The former appear first as wise bridesmaids in Augustine's interpretation of Jesus's parable in the Gospel of Matthew and later as citizens of the city of God; the latter appear as the foolish bridesmaids and later as various heroes and heroines of the Roman Empire. This analysis also returns us to our earlier distinction between performative goodness and communicative goodness because to seek an outer reward often leads to acting for others' applause, while to seek an inner reward from God is an alternative means of recognition. We will identify three marks of a Christian practice of solitude according to St. Augustine: first, an ongoing practice of self-criticism, which includes interrogation of one's motives; second, a strength of conviction that may resist the condemning gaze of others, especially the effects of shame; and, third, freedom to act in ways that may meet with others' disapproval. All of these are supported by a practice of solitude in which the believer dwells alone in the solitude of conscience to engage in dialogue with and before God. We will consider these three marks first by their absence.

Before considering Augustine's interpretation of the parable, it is worth having the details fresh in our mind. Matthew chapter twenty-five records three parables Jesus uses to address the coming of God's kingdom and the nature and criterion of God's future judgment. The first parable concerns wise and foolish bridesmaids (also referred to as virgins). It is worth quoting this key text at length:

> Ten bridesmaids took their lamps and went to meet the bridegroom. Five of them were foolish, and five were wise. When the foolish took their lamps, they took no oil with them; but the wise took flasks of oil with their lamps. As the bridegroom was

delayed, all of them became drowsy and slept. But at midnight there was a shout, "Look! Here is the bridegroom! Come out to meet him." Then all those bridesmaids got up and trimmed their lamps. The foolish said to the wise, "Give us some of your oil, for our lamps are going out." But the wise replied, "No! There will not be enough for you and for us; you had better go to the dealers and buy some for yourselves." And while they went to buy it, the bridegroom came, and those who were ready went with him into the wedding banquet; and the door was shut. Later the other bridesmaids came also, saying, "Lord, lord, open to us." But he replied, "Truly I tell you, I do not know you." Keep awake therefore, for you know neither the day nor the hour.[75]

Augustine's various commentaries on this parable concern the role conscience plays in preparing one for God's final judgment; like Jesus's followers who will await his return after he leaves them, the bridesmaids eagerly await the arrival of the groom to bring them to the wedding feast. While this parable may seem entirely focused on the future, Augustine is interested in how seeking reward outwardly by others' approval or inwardly by conscience makes a difference here and now.

Augustine's reading of the parable remains remarkably consistent from its earliest instance (in *Question 59* from *Miscellany of Eighty-Three Different Questions* written somewhere between 389 and 395) to its latest appearances in his works (in *Sermon 149* delivered somewhere around 412 and 413).[76] He consistently interprets the bridesmaids as people who act with self-restraint, especially in relation to our five senses, thus there are five wise and five foolish virgins; the lamps as their good works; and the oil as the joy they derive from those good works. All the virgins, then, are good, in the sense that they are capable of self-discipline and pursue virtuous actions. The difference between the wise and foolish virgins is between those who determine their actions entirely by others' approval and those who judge themselves in solitude before God: as Augustine writes in his earliest commentary, the foolish act so

---

[75]Mt. 25:1b-13.
[76]He also discusses the parable in *Sermons*, 93; *Letters*, 140; and *Expositions of the Psalms*, 49 and 140.

that "renown might be acquired" while the wise act "to be pleasing to [God] in the inner joy of one's own conscience."[77]

One result of the foolish bridesmaids' reliance on others' approval is that they have never engaged in self-criticism and so cannot give an account of themselves when God requires it at the final judgment. They are unable to give God an account of how and why they acted, because they never engaged in the difficult work of making such decisions themselves. To pursue performative goodness is to act for the sake of your audience's applause. In other words, in determining one's actions entirely by others' approval, one forfeits the responsibility for judging for oneself. The wise bridesmaids cannot give oil to the foolish ones because, at the final judgment, we all stand before God alone. This is not to say that we cannot rely on others' influence in our deliberations. For Augustine the faith and teaching of the church are authoritative. Even so one must consider those influences and deliberate about how they apply in one's own life as one faces particular dilemmas. In a rather comedic scene, Augustine writes that when judged by God, the foolish bridesmaids want to call their usual audience in to answer the questions.[78] The foolish bridesmaids have been so determined by others' seeing of them that apart from others' gaze they have no measure of justification for how they have acted. God's seeing shows how they have forfeited their individual responsibility to think for themselves.

The foolish bridesmaids' desire to have others as one's witnesses at the final judgment reveals another weakness of relying on others' approval: others' seeing of us is decidedly limited, and so their approval may be easier to get. Augustine notes the foolish bridesmaids want witnesses who "do not see the heart," unlike God who does. He makes this point clearly in one of his later interpretations of the parable: "That you do [good works] ... anyone can see; but with what kind of intention you do it only God can see."[79] The foolish bridesmaids lived lives of performance that

[77]Augustine, *Miscellany of Eighty-Three Questions*, trans. Boniface Ramsey, in *Responses to Miscellaneous Questions*, ed. Raymond Canning (New York: New City Press, 2008), 59.3.
[78]Ibid.
[79]*Letters*, 149.12.

avoided examining who they were offstage. Thus even when the foolish bridesmaids occasionally engaged in self-criticism, they left out an evaluation of the desires and motives that were not obvious to others. Augustine maintains that seeking only an outer reward means you apply only outer criteria to your actions; all the foolish virgins care about is what can be seen by others, not what can be seen by God. So seeking only others' approval can be a less-rigorous criterion for one's self-criticism because of their limited perspective.

It is also the case, though, that Augustine thinks that others' judgments may be overly severe and so seeking their approval will finally prove destructive. Audiences don't just applaud, they can "boo" too and often alternate between one or the other and everywhere in between without obvious reasons for doing so. Thus, a third feature of relying on others' approval is how doing so can prove disastrous, especially thanks to the insidious force of shame in which we cannot escape others' condemning gaze. We see this most profoundly in *City of God*, wherein Augustine analyzes how women respond to the horror of rape. In Augustine's day, especially with the decline and fall of the Roman Empire and the instability and chaos that was unleashed, rape was tragically common. In *City*, Augustine distinguishes between two cities and its members; his most famous summation of the cities recalls his earlier comments on the parable of the wise and foolish bridesmaids: "The [city of man] seeks its glory from men, but the [city of God] finds its highest glory in God, the witness of our conscience."[80] Helpfully for our purposes, whereas Augustine's comments on the parable, as we've seen, focus especially on how well-prepared (or not) the women were for God's final judgment, *City of God* has especially in view the consequences for one's life in the world.

Augustine engages with what was apparently regarded as the most virtuous response in the classical Roman world of a woman to her rape: suicide. In his analysis, the classical example of Lucretia's suicide, recorded most famously in Livy's *History of Rome*, demonstrates the most extreme result of depending upon others' approval. The general view at the time was that rape compromised a woman's sexual purity; this included doubts about whether

---

[80]Augustine, *City of God (Books XI–XXII)*, trans. William Babcock (New York: New City Press, 2013), 14.28.

the woman may have in fact been a willing participant or even enjoyed her rape; or, even if neither of the latter were suspected, the woman was still considered tarnished by the man's violation of her. Augustine believes that most regarded Lucretia as innocent, and yet her suicide for the sake of her sexual purity is upheld as admirable. For Augustine, she died not out of a "love of purity," but out of "the weakness of shame."[81] Her dependence on others' approval meant that "she thought she must present her self-punishment to men's eyes in witness to her state of mind, since she could not show them her conscience in itself."[82] In order to overcome the privacy of her conscience, she externalized her remorse by harming herself. This dependence on others' approval for one's own sense of moral stature is dangerous precisely because of the fallibility, selectivity, and severity of others' judgments. He describes how, even when a woman is entirely innocent of wrongdoing when raped, "shame may burst in nonetheless."[83] The vivid language here personifies shame as an actor and a violent actor at that. As Melanie Webb writes, the verb *incutit* ("burst in") "indicates both the immediacy of a bruising blow and the action of causing one to shake, to tremble; after bodies part, shame like a knife rapes the mind and the memory."[84] Thus, the violation to women who have been raped is not only the act itself and its consequences but also the culture of shame that further violates a woman's sense of herself. Depending on others' approval makes one susceptible to this further violation, especially if one already has a marginal or precarious position in society.

One way that this culture of shame applies its pressure is in the examples of women, like Lucretia, who responded to their rape by committing suicide in the name of sexual purity; they were lionized as moral exemplars. As we have already noted, Augustine observed that we are highly imitative animals. We are especially prone to imitate those who are upheld as exemplars. Thus far, we have seen

---

[81]Ibid., 1.19.
[82]Ibid.
[83]Ibid., trans. R. W. Dyson (Cambridge: Cambridge University Press, 1998), 1.16. I use Dyson's translation here because his rendering of the verb "incutit" conforms with Webb's analysis of it, which I go on to discuss.
[84]Melanie Webb, "'On Lucretia who slew herself': Rape and Consolation in Augustine's *De ciuitate dei*," *Augustinian Studies* 44, no. 1 (2013): 53–54.

that Augustine interprets Jesus's command for Christians to do good works publicly as offering an example for others to follow. The converse is that we need to beware of the influence of bad examples. In a letter to a friend, for example, Augustine writes that criminals ought to be dealt with not only in the name of justice but also to not "leave ... a destructive example for others to imitate."[85] City of God in general,[86] and Book 1 in particular,[87] considers the difference that exemplars and the contagious imitation they unleash can make. In particular, Lucretia herself is identified as an exemplar for women.[88] Such examples and those who imitate them serve to further solidify the culture of shame.

A final feature of seeking others' approval is that it tends, in Augustine's analysis, to promote conflict. Augustine believes that conflict can be both necessary and productive, and so he does not think that conflict in and of itself is negative. Yet when conflict seems to be a defining feature of one's life, that may disclose an underlying instability that comes from grasping for others' approval. We see this in City of God, in which the foolish virgins reappear again, but as the heroes of the Roman Empire who act for others' praise. To seek others' approval, Augustine believes, will tend to provoke conflict because a highly effective way to earn your audience's applause is by emerging as a hero of some battle or other. In order to see this, Augustine engages in a whole-scale analysis of Roman culture. In the first ten chapters of City, he seeks to demonstrate that contrary to those who criticized Christians for the fall of the Roman Empire, the instability that led to the empire's collapse was inherent to it. Central to his argument is interrogating the results of acting for others' approval, which Augustine judges was the foundation of Roman culture. After he establishes in chapters one through four that the success of the Roman Empire did not depend on the support of their gods, he turns in chapter five to discuss the role that Roman virtue played in that success. He enlists the aid

---

[85]*Letters 1–99*, trans. Roland Teske (New York: New City Press, 2001), 91.6.

[86]I pursue this topic in greater depth in my article "Imitation and the Mediation of Christ in Augustine's *City of God*," *Studia Patristica*, no. 70 (2013): 449–455.

[87]Augustine does so with reference to particular examples in *City of God*, namely Regulus (1.15) and Romulus and Remus (1.34); he also contrasts imitation with reason (1.22).

[88]Ibid., 1.19.3.

of many Roman authors to demonstrate that what drove Romans above all else was the love for glory, which Augustine defines as "the judgment of men thinking well of other men." He writes:

> It was for [glory's] sake that they wanted to live and for its sake that they did not hesitate to die. Their boundless desire for this one thing kept all their other desires in check. In short, since they considered it shameful for their country to serve, but glorious for it to dominate and rule, what they desire with all their hearts was first for it to be free and then for it to be dominant.[89]

Augustine defines the ordering principle of the Roman Empire: the Romans pursue freedom and mastery for the sake of glory. They are consummate performers, acting to display their goodness.

Augustine's analysis acknowledges the positive results of acting for others' approval. For one thing, when you are constantly aware of how others might see you, that fosters certain actions and curbs others.[90] You end up crafting yourself to earn the approval of your audience, and so the virtues they value are likely to appear in you.[91] We recall in the last chapter that Jesus says that those who seek the reward of others' approval will receive it by often earning the recognition that they desire. Augustine interprets this in terms of the positive results that may come from seeking others' approval.[92] The most obvious example of this is the unprecedented success of the Roman Empire: "They were honored among almost all nations; they imposed the laws of their empire on many peoples; and even today they are glorious among almost all peoples in history and literature. They have no grounds for complaint against the justice of the supreme and true God: *they have received their reward.*"[93] Augustine does not dismiss, then, how the desire for approval furnishes success of all kinds, as the Roman Empire was a model of political, ethical, and artistic accomplishment. The rewards the

---

[89]*City of God (Books I–X)*, trans. William Babcock (New York: New City Press, 2012), 5.12.
[90]Ibid., 5.13.
[91]Ibid., 5.19.
[92]See, for example, *Sermons*, 137.11 and 138.1.
[93]*City of God*, 5.15.

Romans received for their love of glory fill the history books and continue to inspire admiration and awe.

Augustine hastens to add, though, that the love of glory is the source of both the Roman Empire's success and its imperialism and violence. Once they had achieved the glory of their own freedom, the Romans then sought mastery over others.[94] Glory depends on the number of spectators and on their witnessing great deeds. Thus, Augustine sees the love of glory as essential to the logic of empire, which keeps expanding, often through oppression and violence. Augustine notes that the expansion of the Roman Empire could perhaps have occurred without violence or at least involved far less violence than it did; yet, he notes wryly, "No one is victor where no one has fought."[95] The desire for glory, in other words, includes a certain propensity toward conflict, so that you can continue to receive the adulation you crave by emerging the valiant victor. As well, you might also be in search of more and more audiences, which adds a further momentum. Eventually, Augustine thinks, this endless need for expansion and conflict is not sustainable. Both the success and savagery of the Roman Empire, then, are tied to the desire for glory, the pursuit of performative goodness; and so, its success also inexorably leads to its destruction. Performative goodness, then, forms one to be competitive, as often one needs to engage in conflict or rivalry to hear the applause or to garner the loudest applause for oneself.

To seek the outer reward of others' approval, then, in Augustine's analysis, may lead to forfeiting one's responsibility to think for oneself, applying a less-rigorous self-criticism, succumbing to the destructive force of shame, and pursuing conflict. We are now ready to see how the wise bridesmaids and their counterparts in the *City of God* differ because they seek the inner reward of God's approval within the solitude of their consciences. We shall supplement Augustine's commentary on the parable and *City* with what he says elsewhere about conscience.

To start, the wise virgins act "to be pleasing to [God] in the inner joy of ... conscience."[96] Or, as he puts it in a later interpretation, we

---

[94]Ibid., 5.11.
[95]Ibid., 5.17.
[96]*Miscellany of Eighty-Three Different Questions*, 59.3.

ought to follow the wise virgins and "carry [the oil] inside, where God can see; carry the testimony of your conscience there."[97] The first difference, then, is that the wise virgins' sense of being viewed by God means that they constantly turn within to engage in the ongoing work of self-criticism. The first step of this process involves attending to one's conscience: "Come back to your conscience."[98] That he advises us to "come back" to our consciences indicates that departing from our consciences involves a kind of alienation from ourselves. As Sorabji explained above, conscience generally involves a sense of oneself as involving a duality, such that one part of me can know what another refuses to admit. And so, Augustine says: "Go back into yourself, pay attention to yourself, examine yourself, listen to yourself."[99] When we do "listen," one role that conscience plays in our dialogue with ourselves is that of an interrogator. As Augustine describes a painful turning point in his own life: "I was stripped naked in my own eyes and my conscience challenged me within: 'Where is your ready tongue now?'"[100] This sense of interrogation is expanded in his description of entering one's conscience as engaging in a kind of legal trial; conscience is prosecuting the case.[101] But conscience is also called on as witness: "Let your conscience bear you witness."[102] And conscience serves as judge: "Let him enter into himself, ascend the judgement-seat of his own mind."[103] The diverse roles that conscience can play illustrates the conversational dynamic of this practice of solitude. When engaged in a genuinely searching moral self-examination, conscience will play a variety of roles, of prosecution, witness, judge, and defense. This underlines how consistent withdrawal into conscience will demand that one provide, to and for oneself, a justification for how one acts. Our capacity for dialogue with ourselves about who we are and how we act, so nicely explained by Arendt, Augustine believes, is motivated by belief in a God who

---

[97]*Sermons (51–94)*, trans. Edmund Hill (New York: New City Press, 1991), 93.10.
[98]*Sermons (1–19)*, 13.6.6.
[99]Ibid., 13.6.7.
[100]*Confessions*, trans. Maria Boulding (New York: New City Press, 2007), 8. 7. 18.
[101]*Expositions of the Psalms*, 57.2.
[102]*Homilies on the First Epistle of John*, 6.3.
[103]*Homilies on the Gospel of John*, trans. Edmund Hill (New York: New City Press, 2009), 33.5.

always sees us and will ultimately demand we give an account of ourselves. And so, the wise virgins are prepared—or, at least, more prepared—for God's judgment. Augustine notes that their consciences were "bearing good witness for them before God."[104] Whereas the foolish virgins seek other human beings as their witnesses, the wise virgins have their consciences. The wise virgins can give an account of themselves to God at the final judgment, for, in effect, they have been doing so in the solitude of their consciences throughout their lives.

Further, when we turn within to the privacy of our conscience, we do so in the belief that God can see where others can't, and that may, Augustine believes, promote a more rigorous self-evaluation. It is not the case, then, that self-judgment by conscience is a practice in which we strike off by ourselves to revel in our glorious individuality. Rather, I still seek the approval of an other, but in this case I do so by considering how God sees me. Augustine frequently emphasizes how conscience is an intimate space of encounter with God. God serves as another witness to one's deliberations and reflections, along with conscience: "My own conscience ... and the God who dwells in pure souls are my witness."[105] God has a privileged place as the only other companion with you in your solitude, that inner desert "where no other human being gains entry, where no one is with you, where there is only yourself and God."[106] And God alone is the only truly reliable judge, whatever one's own conscience may conclude: "Is my recollection not accurate, Lord God, judge of my conscience? My heart and my memory of these things lie open before you."[107] In one example, when Augustine reminds his congregation of God's presence to them, he does so in order to promote reflection on their actions *and* motivations: "You are before God: question your heart, see what you have done, and what therein was your aim."[108] In the latter quotation, Augustine advises us to expose to ourselves and God not just what we did but also what we wanted

---

[104]*Miscellany of Eighty-Three Different Questions*, 59.3.
[105]*The Advantage of Believing*, trans. Ray Kearney, in *On Christian Belief*, ed. Boniface Ramsay (New York: New City Press, 2005), 6.13.
[106]*Expositions of the Psalms*, 54.9.
[107]*Confessions*, 5.6.11.
[108]*Homilies on the First Epistle of John*, 6.2.

from our actions. Thus, this awareness of God's complete seeing of us, in Augustine's mind, demands we not hide from ourselves the complex desires that may be at work.

In particular, Augustine believes that the Christian should interrogate herself about whether, however her actions may have appeared, she actually acted out of love. Love is defined for Augustine by Jesus's command to love others "as ourselves," in other words, as equals under God. This sense of equality is one distinctive feature of the pursuit of communicative goodness: to see oneself as the recipient of God's love, a criterion of one's self-criticism is how well that same loving is being communicated to those we are to treat as equals. We shall consider this at greater length in the next chapter. For now, we note that Augustine often describes how God's gift of faith inspires an ongoing interrogation about the character of one's love. Thus even as you retreat from others to the "desert" of your conscience, in that private space the believer is to "interrogate our faith. Let us ask if there is love there inside."[109] The primary object of one's moral judgment, then, is to discern whether we act out of love or its opposite: "Examine yourselves ... Let love be born in you if it hasn't been born yet, and if it has, let it be fed and nourished, let it grow ... so let love increase, greed decrease, so that one day ... love, may be perfected, greed may be wiped out."[110] Ongoing attention to whether one acts out of love or greed is not a mere obsession with motives; as we shall see in the next chapter, Augustine believes that often at work in us, though unacknowledged, are envy and anger, which can be suppressed for some time, but will eventually disclose themselves in our relationships with others. Thus, rigorous self-examination about one's motives may actually be a means to love others better. Plumbing the depths of one's desires and motivations, he thinks, is facilitated by a belief that God sees them, so we ought to do our best to see them too.

Thankfully, Augustine pairs the potential rigor of Christians' self-judgment with their faith that God's looking at them is also defined by compassion. God does not only act in our consciences as witness, judge, and interlocutor, then. When we acknowledge our

---

[109]*Sermons (20–50)*, 47.23.
[110]*Sermons (51–94)*, 90.6.

wrongdoing, Augustine pictures God as becoming "intercessor."[111] He associates this especially with the role of the Son, who intercedes for human sin. As Augustine writes of the tax-collector in Jesus's parable: "He took the role of judge over himself so that the Lord might be the intercessor; he was punishing himself so that another might set him free; he was accusing himself so that the other might defend him."[112] Acknowledgment of wrongdoing may increase one's intimacy with God by underlining our need for God. As Augustine advises his congregation, "in order to become good call upon the One who is good."[113] This posture of calling upon God restores one's creaturely dependence on God. To attempt to hide from oneself and God one's wrongdoing is a delusional fantasy: "I would be hiding you from myself, but not myself from you."[114] By contrast, confession to God in "groans" shows that, apart from God, the self is at odds with itself, and instead the integrity of our personhood lies in our dependence on God. As Augustine continues, after he confesses, "you shed light upon me and give me joy, you offer yourself, lovable and longed for, that I may thrust myself away in disgust and choose you, and be pleasing no more either to you or to myself except in what I have from you."[115] This defines the gaze of God within, then, as ultimately a compassionate gaze, supporting us to be truthful about ourselves and empowering us to always begin again.

And it is trust in that boundless compassion that puts a limit to the possibility of obsessive self-scrutiny. Augustine is not confident, for himself or any of us, that even the most devoted practice of self-criticism will ever spot all the wrongs we have done. To think that we could ever attain such transparency to ourselves is the height of delusion: "Each person is hardly sufficient in himself so that his own conscience might bear witness for him. In fact, who will boast that he has a pure heart?"[116] Yet faith orients us here, too, for Augustine

---

[111]*Expositions of the Psalms (1–32)*, trans. Edmund Hill (New York: New City Press, 2000), second exposition of 31.12.

[112]Ibid.

[113]*Sermons (1–19)*, 13.6.6.

[114]*Confessions*, 10.2.2.

[115]Ibid.

[116]*Miscellany of Eighty-Three Different Questions*, 59.3.

believes in a God who both knows and loves us completely: "God
... knows in us even what we know not in ourselves ... So there
are some things then that God is aware of in us which we do not
know about."[117] Thus our hope lies not in our own transparency
to ourselves, but instead, he writes, we are "more secure in our
hope of your mercy than in [our consciences'] own innocence."[118]
Augustine certainly does emphasize, as we have seen, our ongoing
need for self-criticism in solitude where God alone can see us. While
our awareness of God's seeing us certainly encourages rigor where
Augustine thinks we might otherwise be lax, God's seeing may also
serve to halt an obsessive tendency to endlessly scrutinize ourselves.
By turning to God in solitude, we entrust ourselves to one who both
knows and loves us completely.

Implicit in what has been said so far is a fundamental contrast
between the wise and foolish bridesmaids that turns out to be
especially crucial in the cultural analysis of *City of God*: the wise
virgins' turn to the solitude of conscience facilitates an independent
perspective on themselves and the influences that form them. To be
run primarily by others' approval means that we will reflect whatever
consensus or convention is followed by the majority or tribe whose
recognition we seek; we saw above the tragic consequences of this
for women in the Roman Empire who committed suicide in order
to demonstrate their commitment to sexual purity. To turn "within"
where I can be alone before God is to seek to get some perspective
on others' influences and to pursue God's recognition. Such
perspective does not necessarily mean that I reject others' views;
instead, I take responsibility for thinking through those views for
myself. It is precisely the inaccessibility of my conscience to others
that affords me an alternative view of my action from the one that
I see reflected back at me in the eyes of others. This can include, as
we have already seen, a more rigorous evaluation of myself than
what would earn others' approval. It could equally be, though, that
I refuse to see wrong, or refuse to evaluate the wrong I have done,
as severely as others do.

The significance of developing a self-evaluation that is
independent of others' influence is explored most strikingly in

---

[117]*Homilies on the Gospel of John*, 32.5.
[118]*Confessions*, 10.3.4.

City of God, when our wise virgins reappear as Christian women who survive rape and do not commit suicide. When he first raises the subject of rape in *City of God*, Augustine notes that Christian women too are being raped, including married, single, and celibate women. He specifies that he is writing less to criticize pagans and more in order "to comfort our own." No doubt Augustine includes in "our own" women who have themselves been raped. According to Webb, with his reference to "comfort," Augustine is indicating that he is engaging in a particular genre of writing, in which one offers consolation to a person or group of people who have suffered.[119] There are many examples of this genre in the ancient world for people who suffer from exile and grief. Disturbingly, Webb finds no other example, among pagans or Christians, of an author who writes to woman who have suffered rape.[120] Augustine is innovating.

Augustine offers comfort based on the nature of Christian conscience. He contrasts Lucretia's suicide with the conduct of Christian women: "They have the glory of chastity within them, the witness of conscience. They have this in the eyes of God, and they need nothing more."[121] The testimony of conscience, then, provides a stability that counters others' disapproval; this stability arises from conscience's place "in the eyes of God," no matter how others may disapprove or condemn. Having engaged in a close examination of the nature and role of conscience for Augustine, we have an enlarged sense of what that "testimony of their own conscience" involves. Augustine has in mind conscience as a private inner space where one can engage in dialogue before and with God. In this case, Augustine believes that Christian women's refusal of suicide comes from their conclusion that they did nothing wrong and, further, from also experiencing God's approval "within." The privacy of their conscience and the support of God that they experience there offer a much-needed protection against the culturally sanctioned notion of sexual purity. We also note Augustine's use of this metaphor of God's seeing. The Christian women define themselves

---

[119]Webb, "'On Lucretia who slew herself': Rape and Consolation in Augustine's *De ciuitate dei*," 55.

[120]Ibid., 57.

[121]*City of God*, 1.19.

not in terms of their sense of how others see them but how God sees them. God's seeing of them in solitude empowers them to disregard the condemning gaze of others.

The consequence of Christian women's countercultural refusal of suicide after rape is not only a victory for each of them as individuals, though it certainly is that. They also serve to provide alternative examples that can be imitated. Thus, the result of their interiority actually has consequences that extend far beyond themselves. Every Christian woman who does not commit suicide after surviving rape makes it that much easier for future women to resist the culture of shame.

This brings us to the final difference Augustine identifies between seeking others' approval without and pursuing God's approval within. As we saw above, Augustine believes that seeking others' approval can promote competition and conflict that ultimately undermine mutuality and community. Because the Christian's conscience is marked by faith in God, Augustine believes it is a space of hope, hope that is defined by expectation that God is already at work to bring about a universal human community grounded in the communicative goodness of God. A bad conscience, Augustine thinks, can be a place of despair. To "suffer from a bad conscience" is to be "estranged ... from hope" because you fear, perhaps not even consciously, God's judgment, which your conscience already, if only dimly, anticipates.[122] By contrast, hope, as he puts it pithily in a sermon, is "the sign of at least some goodness of conscience."[123] That good conscience comes from faith and love, which he characterizes as "belief and work."[124] It is especially when the Christian examines her conscience and discovers love at work in her that hope comes from a good conscience: "Now when people perform good actions their love endows them with the hope that proceeds from a good conscience ... a good conscience fills us entirely with hope."[125]

Most importantly for us, Augustine also identifies our conscience as a private place in which we hope for the final overturning of all privacy that will usher in full communion between one another and

---

God. Solitude, as I mentioned in the Introduction, is a temporary and remedial practice for Augustine. In one sermon, he writes that within the desert of our conscience we can retreat and there "rest in hope," and this hope is specifically for when "we shall finally be transparent to each other ... And our consciences will not be a desert or solitude, because everyone will be known to each other and will not have their thoughts unknown."[126] This description is an essential feature of Augustine's view of what heaven will be like, grounded as it is in his interpretation of Scripture. In the stunning final chapters of *City of God*, he describes the perfected sight that human beings will have as better than "certain serpents or eagles are reported to see" for they "only see corporeal things." Rather we will even be able to see "incorporeal things."[127] Augustine readily admits that such a state is essentially impossible to conceive of now, but he speculates about what it will be like. Our perfected vision will see God "with brilliant clarity, everywhere present and governing all things, including bodily things—seeing him both through the bodies we shall be wearing and through the bodies we shall be looking at." He goes on to detail the implications of our seeing God *everywhere*, including that we will be able to see one another's thoughts.[128] With this perfected vision, the distinction between inner and outer vanishes entirely and forever to enable perfect communion. Yet in this sermon that distinction, for now, persists. The solitude of our conscience is at once lauded as a place of retreat *and* marked as a space where we hope for its eventual dissolution in the perfected community of creatures and Creator. To seek God's approval within, then, is a means of preparing oneself for that community; this is in contrast to seeking others' approval without, which often serves to facilitate conflict and competition for the finite resource of others' adulation.

Conclusion

By way of concluding this chapter, we return briefly to Plotinus's influence on Augustine. We have seen that so much of what

---

[126]*Sermons (20–50)*, 47.23.
[127]*City of God*, 22.29.
[128]Ibid.

Augustine regards as distinguishing a Christian practice of solitude comes from the belief that we have an inner space within us where God alone can see. That belief facilitates ongoing self-criticism, a self-criticism that may be more rigorous because God can see where others can't or may empower us to not be violated by the shame at work in our culture, but to trust instead in God's complete and compassionate seeing of us. Earlier in this chapter we saw that Augustine's depiction of conscience as an inner space reflects the influence of Plotinus's first level of divine transcendence, specifically the divine Mind that thinks the ideas of things, to which we have access within our souls. In depicting this space as a place where God sees us as individuals, Augustine rejects Plotinus's second level of transcendence.

What is this "second level" of transcendence? Plotinus breaks with some in his Platonic tradition, though he regarded himself as staying true to Plato, in distinguishing between the transcendent level of the ideas and a still higher level of transcendence occupied by the ultimate divine principle, the One. Plotinus's innovation is to distinguish the ideas from the One. Plotinus does so, quite simply, by arguing that the One is not a mind or endowed with intelligence; while there is a divine Mind that does think the ideas of all things, that is not the highest divinity. To say that the highest divinity thinks is to associate it too closely with the finite, as thinking involves objects of thought and therefore implies division between a subject and object. To protect the One's transcendence, in other words, we must deny so much of what we might piously associate with divinity, for, Plotinus writes, the One is "not a 'this', nor quality or quantity, neither Intellect nor Soul. Neither is it in motion nor at a standstill, nor in place or time, but ... it is formless, being prior to all Form, prior to Motion and Stability."[129]

To distinguish the world from the One in some way would be to ascribe some definable, and therefore finite, attribute to the One; in other words, describing a separation between the One and the world, perhaps out of a desire for philosophical precision or religious piety, turns out to be a false start. As Kenney explains: "The One must be understood to be fundamental, indeed so fundamental that it cannot even be seen primarily in terms of its

---

[129]Plotinus, *The Enneads*, 6.9.3.

distinction from the world. To do so would be to draw the One into a relation with the world, making the One, as it were, part of a larger system."[130] This indicates clearly why Plotinus is so prone to the use of paradox, and the central paradox, according to Kenney, is that "the One was entirely hidden and intensely present, transcendent of all predicates and yet the immediate ground of all finite being."[131] This understanding of divine transcendence locates the divine in its very transcendence, paradoxically, as immediately and intimately present to all that is.

What is most essential for us is that Plotinus thinks it is incompatible with the One's transcendence to pray to the One in the way that Augustine thinks we should do when we are alone before God in conscience. Kenney identifies a number of reasons this is so. For our purposes, we will focus on two. First of all, Plotinus's key move, in which he departs from many of his ancient predecessors, is to say that the One is not a mind that possesses intelligence, it is beyond intelligence. That second level of transcendence, then, neither literally nor figuratively, may be said to attend to or address human beings as individuals, nor is there any sense in human beings entering into dialogue with or before the One. There are other, lesser, deities to whom one can pray, but not the One. Second, the One being beyond intelligence also means that it is not paying attention to individuals; we are not an object of the One's particular consideration. This further underlines a misunderstanding of the transcendence of the One.[132]

Augustine rejects Plotinus's second level of transcendence because Augustine's God is not only a transcendent intelligence but an intelligence that knows and attends to each of us as an individual. We saw in the last chapter how God's personal seeing of us is a feature of the biblical tradition. In rejecting Plotinus's second level of transcendence, then, Augustine is siding with this biblical tradition. And yet, his own particular appropriation of Plotinus's sense of inner space locates that seeing of God as occurring within, so that each of us has the private inner space of our conscience. Through Augustine's complex engagement with Plotinus's

---

[130]Kenney, *Contemplation and Classical Christianity*, 15.
[131]Ibid., 19.
[132]Ibid., 20–21, 38, 49.

influence, he has crafted a particular approach to Christian solitude that puts this roomy sense of inner spaciousness at the service of ongoing dialogue with and before God. That dialogue facilitates an alternative view of oneself than what is on offer by myself alone or the approval of others. In the next chapter, we will pursue further how such a practice of solitude can alter not only how I see myself but how I see others too.

3

The Publicity of Love

No one after lighting a lamp puts it under the bushel
basket, but on the lampstand, and it gives light to all
the house. In the same way, let your light shine before
others, so that they may see your good works and give
glory to your Father in heaven.

—MATTHEW 5:15-16

Jesus instructs his followers that after they retreat from the world into their inner room to pray, their first words should be "Our Father." I argued in second chapter that this "our" defines the Christian, even when she is alone, as a member of a "we" whose prayer is marked by constant reference to membership in that "we". Rather than an antisocial solitude, then, the Sermon on the Mount depicts a Christian practice of solitude as a means of resocialization. In one of his comments on these first words of the Lord's Prayer, Augustine marvels that Jesus, Son of God, "thought it proper to have brothers and sisters."[1] By instructing his followers to pray to God as Father, he is inviting all to share the intimate companionship with God that he enjoys. Another implication of saying those words is the "all-embracing generosity" of God toward humanity, as "the emperor says ['Our Father'], the beggar says it; the slave says it, his master says it ... So they must realize that they are brothers, since they all have one Father."[2] To pray this prayer in

---

[1] *Sermons (51–94)*, trans. Edmund Hill (New York: New City Press, 1991), 57.2.
[2] Ibid., 58.2.

solitude is to depict oneself as a sibling with all of humanity. And, as I also argued in the second chapter, it also focuses repeatedly on our common neediness, which we might do our best to obscure in our relationships with others. The companionship of God in solitude may serve to transform the companionship we offer others when we go public. As we continue to explore Augustine as an inheritor and interpreter of Jesus's teaching on solitude, we now examine how Augustine sees the relation between solitude and community.

To start, even as we ought to regularly withdraw from the world into solitude, Augustine does not take that to mean we abandon all thought of others. Instead, he sees withdrawal as an opportunity to interrogate oneself about one's relations to others. The primary question we are to put to ourselves, as we touched on in the last chapter, concerns what and how we love: "Let us come back then to conscience ... Therefore, let each one of us 'prove his own work' whether it flow from the vein of love, whether it be from love as the root that his good works sprout as branches ... not when another's tongue bears witness to him, but when his conscience bears it."[3] By love Augustine has in mind here not romantic attraction or a vague warm-and-fuzzy feeling toward others but a love that is grounded in a knowledge of the way things really are. True love, Augustine thinks, is a response of the lover to seeing what is good about the beloved. But it's often the case that love is bound up with an inaccurate or even deluded perception of the beloved. So Augustine makes a crucial distinction between a discerning love, which recognizes and responds to a good that is really there, and distorted love, which depends on some false good or other that is projected or imagined onto the other. Augustine even goes so far as to say that "a just and holy life" requires that we make accurate judgments about the way things are[4] and love accordingly: "so that you do not love what is not to be loved, or fail to love what is to be loved, or have a greater love for what should be loved less, or an equal love for things that should be loved less or more, or a lesser or greater love

[3]*Homilies on the First Epistle of John*, trans. Boniface Ramsey (New York: New City Press, 2008), 6.2.
[4]I follow Ian Clausen in translating Augustine's often used phrase *ordo rerum* as "the way things are"; see Ian Clausen, "Seeking the Place of Conscience in Higher Education: An Augustinian View," 287.

for things that should be loved equally."[5] The reference to equality in this quotation is especially relevant for us because when it comes to our self-examination, a recurring question Augustine advises that we put to ourselves is whether we love others as equals. To love another more than myself—or less than myself—is to fail to love with a discerning love.

The remainder of this chapter will consist in tracing out the implications of this discerning love for a Christian practice of solitude. We shall do so by referring again to our distinction between performative goodness and communicative goodness. Recall that one who acts according to performative goodness relentlessly pursues others' approval, and so they regard themselves as the star of their lives and others serve as their audience; one who is gradually freeing herself from a need for others' approval can act instead according to communicative goodness, in which one regards oneself first and foremost as a recipient of God's goodness and further seeks to reflect that goodness by making it available to others. Especially important for us is that judging oneself in terms of communicative goodness demands paying attention to two directions in which goodness can move. One direction, as just mentioned, is that in which I regard myself as receiving goodness from God and then mediating it to others. The other direction is to attend to others as themselves communicators of God's goodness. For Augustine, the fullest realization of this comes from Christians who, by the healing work of God in the faith and life of the church, are gradually being reformed to God's image. Apart from one's faith or church-membership, though, Augustine believes that any and all human beings who exist—merely in virtue of their existing— communicate something of God's goodness. To apply this belief to a practice of self-criticism in solitude, in the first section of this chapter we shall see how the primary question we are to put to ourselves in our conscience is whether we are communicating God's goodness, specifically in terms of love. With this in mind, Augustine thinks we do need to pay some attention to our reputations as a means of loving others, though we ought also be ready to sacrifice our reputation for others' good. This conforms to the movement of

---

[5]Augustine, *Teaching Christianity*, trans. Edmund Hill (New York: New City Press, 2014), 1.27.28.

goodness from God to me and then onward to others. In the second section, we trace the movement of goodness in the other way. Thus I ought also to interrogate myself about whether I attend to all others—emphasis on the *all*—as communicators of God's goodness. Augustine has practical advice to give about how we can better see others in that way. To support the latter argument, I shall enlist the aid of another great literary work, Marilynne Robinson's *Gilead*.

Mediating goodness to others

We saw in the last chapter that the practice of solitude in the privacy of conscience may give us an alternative perspective on ourselves; instead of relying primarily on others' seeing of us, we may retreat within to attend to how God sees us. This practice may demand that our self-examination be more rigorous than it would be otherwise; likewise it may serve to protect us from the destructive effects of shame. Yet Augustine also argues that this independent perspective on ourselves does not give us license to act without concern for others' opinions. Love demands, Augustine thinks, that we consider how we appear to others. When, for example, I have concluded that something others regard as immoral I take to be moral, I cannot disregard the opinions of others out of brazen confidence that God is on my side. Love integrates the privacy of conscience with my role in public. Following Paul, Augustine believes that even if we conclude in the privacy of our conscience that some act is entirely acceptable, we may want to lovingly abstain from it when we are with others who judge it to be immoral. Augustine sees in Paul's letters three reasons to abstain from food or drink: first, in order to avoid overindulging; second, to prevent others from coming into contact with pagan rituals; or, third, "what is most praiseworthy of all, from love, not to offend the weakness of those more feeble than ourselves, who abstain from these things."[6] In later interpretations of Paul's teaching, Augustine is even more emphatic that our good conscience cannot lead us to disregard the sensitivities of others,

---

[6]*The Catholic Way of Life and the Manichean Way of Life*, trans. Roland Teske, in *The Manichean Debate* (New York: New City Press, 2006), 2.14.33.

especially the sensitivities of those who are very well intentioned, but vulnerable and so liable to be scandalized if a member of their community acts contrary to what they regard as right. Even if I am assured that I am right and another is in error, it remains the case that my love of myself cannot oppose itself to love of another.[7]

Such care for others includes watching out for your reputation not because you act for others' approval but because your public persona has an influence on others. A human life often functions as a sign for others that, whether we intend to or not, is often communicating something. So claiming that you can disregard others' opinions because you have a clear conscience before God is illegitimate, Augustine thinks. This kind of saintly machismo that disregards, perhaps even invites, others' disapproval is a misuse of the privacy of conscience. Caring for one's reputation, in so far as this is possible, is part of loving your neighbor: "The person who shields his life from evil or shameful accusations does good to himself, but he who also protects his reputation shows mercy to others."[8] And so, regardless of what the testimony of my conscience may say, in order to love my neighbor, I must attend to my public persona for the sake of the community. Thus we see that love of the other, for Augustine, involves a sort of holy public relations. I am responsible for tending to my reputation as it plays a role in what my life is communicating.

This responsibility for one's reputation may include crafting one's life as an example for imitation. We saw in the previous chapter that Augustine praises Christian women who survive rape and do not commit suicide as providing an alternative example for other women who survive rape. He encourages them for how they are building an alternative culture, in which suffering rape is not a cause of shame. They need to disregard the approval of those with a false concept of female sexual purity, but they do so in the hopes of influencing others who want to reject that shame too. Acting as an exemplar is, Augustine thinks, what Jesus had in mind when he commanded his followers to be salt and light in the Sermon on the

---

[7]*Sermons*, 3.3, 62.4.7, and 82.3.4.
[8]*The Excellence of Widowhood*, trans. M. Clement Eagan, in *Treatises on Various Subjects*, ed. Roy J. Deferrari (New York: The Fathers of the Church Inc., 1952), 22.27.

Mount.[9] As Augustine advised his congregation: "If you are afraid that people will see you, you will have no imitators; therefore you should be seen. But that isn't why you should allow yourself to be seen. The goal of your joy mustn't be there."[10] Given that we are such fiercely imitative animals, others need good examples as models, especially those who are still developing the ability to judge for themselves.[11] While Augustine believes that the goal for every Christian is to be able to come to her own judgment, imitation is a means to develop that capacity.[12]

This does not mean that if we attend to the kind of public example we are setting we necessarily will do our best to present ourselves as perfect. Augustine's own example in *Confessions* demonstrates otherwise. That text is one of the most—if not the most—personally revealing publications written to that point. He is not intending to write a contemporary salacious tell-all memoir, though there is certainly a great deal of the fifth-century equivalent of drugs, sex, and rock-and-roll. Instead, if we take the example of his life that he crafts of himself, we see that not depending on others' approval may actually free us up to be vulnerable with them, to share with others, in a raw and penetrating way, when we have failed. The form *Confessions* takes, we should not be surprised, is a dialogue before and with God, in which the readers are generally present as those who are privileged to overhear this often brutally honest and searching conversation. In this way, the Psalms is clearly one inspiration for the form *Confessions* takes. As Augustine writes: "I can say nothing right to other people unless you have heard it from me first, nor can you even hear anything of the kind from me which you have not first told me."[13] Augustine is willing to describe his failures and frailties in the hopes that others will benefit from over-hearing them. This selective openness may serve as a particular trademark of communicative goodness.

---

[9]Augustine, *The Lord's Sermon on the Mount*, 1.6.17.
[10]*Homilies on the First Epistle of John*, 6.3.
[11]*Confessions*, 13.21.31.
[12]Much of Augustine's criticism of his education in *Confessions* and of the Roman theatre in *City of God* concern the destructive examples they provided (intentionally or not) for imitation; see *Confessions* 1.18.28–1.19.30 and *City* 4.1, 9.15, 9.21.
[13]*Confessions*, 10.2.2.

Having thus far seen how evaluating oneself in terms of discerning love will involve caring for one's reputation, we now must also consider how it may demand instead a willingness to sacrifice it. This sacrifice may be required when, Augustine thinks, not acting for others' approval may give you the freedom to act in ways that others genuinely need. If my action is motivated primarily by seeking others' approval, I am impaired in my ability to genuinely love them. In other words, self-criticism in the privacy of conscience can gradually reorder me from a constant seeking of others' approval to attending instead to others' genuine needs. Thus, the very privacy of self-examination results in a properly public action: not one that has my ego's need to be liked as its end, but rather another's well-being. The relation to neighbor that responds to genuine need and seeks the good of all is in stark contrast to that which sees others primarily as members of my audience whose applause I constantly seek. We saw in the last chapter that Augustine believes the Roman heroes' desire for glory demands others see them as superior; thus even when the Roman Empire granted citizenship to others outside its initial territory, it was granted not by persuasion but by imposition, including the use of violence. The Roman heroes needed to be seen as conquerors in order that they could receive glory.[14] Augustine's description of the Christian apostles is clearly in contrast to these Roman heroes, and it involves precisely the kind of love that he ties to a practice of self-examination alone before God. Augustine emphasizes how the apostles proclaimed their faith to all people even when they were well aware of the hatred and persecution it would cause. What determined their evangelism was that they believed others needed to hear it.[15] The apostles acted to make their faith a public communication in order that there might be a universal fellowship. Such actions were dependent upon freedom from concern for others' approval.[16]

---

[14]*City of God*, 5.17.

[15]Ibid., 5.15.

[16]Rowan Williams argues, against Hannah Arendt, that rather than destroying any notion of the public in *City of God*, Augustine "is engaged in a redefinition of the public itself, designed to show that it is life outside the Christian community which fails to be truly public, authentically political"; see "Politics and the Soul: A Reading of the *City of God*," *Milltown Studies* no. 19.12 (1987): 58.

Another example of the difference freedom from others' approval can make has to do with how to respond to wrongdoing. In his correspondence with civil and episcopal authorities, Augustine is concerned that they are feeling extreme public pressure to be "tough on crime" (sound familiar?).[17] According to Augustine's theology, civil judges have a God-given duty to use punishment to instill fear in those who would break the law in order to maintain order[18]; and criminals' freedom should be restrained in order that they not commit further crimes.[19] He refers to this as taking part in God's "providential care" of the world.[20] Even so, he advises them to exercise restraint and keep in mind "Christian gentleness"[21] by which they would limit the severity of their punishment to what is necessary to keep order in society and facilitate the criminal's reform.[22] Whatever punishment is applied should not take away the criminals' "life and bodily integrity," but should serve "their benefit and well-being."[23] Exercising this kind of restraint in punishing criminals threatens to earn one a reputation for being a bleeding-heart softy.

But before we bleeding-heart softies indulge in too much self-congratulation that Augustine is on our side, we should note that he also advises that freedom from needing others' approval may also require severity when such is deemed necessary. Augustine's consistency, it seems to me, is admirable; if we desire a reputation for severity, it may get in the way when responding gently is more useful, and so too if we a desire a reputation for gentleness, that may get in the way when severity is appropriate. We see the relation between conscience and a capacity for necessary severity in his *Homilies on the First Epistle of John*. First, Augustine calls his

---

[17]Robert Dodaro helpfully provides the historical background of these letters and discusses what they reveal about Augustine as a "political activist"; see "Between the Two Cities: Political Action in Augustine of Hippo," in *Augustine and Politics*, ed. John Doody, Kevin L. Hughes, and Kim Paffenroth (New York: Lexington Books, 2005), 99–116.

[18]*Letters*, 100.1.

[19]Ibid., 133.1.

[20]Ibid., 104.3.9.

[21]Ibid., 91, 100, 133, and 139.

[22]Ibid., 91.7.

[23]Ibid., 91.7, 95.3, and 100.1.

listeners to engage in self-judgment: "Scripture inwardly beckons us away from the boastfulness of this appearance outwardly, and from that surface which boasts in the presence of men it beckons us to what is within. Return to your conscience; question it."[24] Next, he proceeds to connect the importance of self-criticism "within" to the claim that love may sometimes need to be severe: "The proud man flatters; love is severe … Go within, then, brothers, and in everything, whatever you may do, glimpse God as your witness."[25] Acting entirely according to others' approval may cause us to avoid the need to be severe out of love. Thus in the privacy of conscience, with God alone as our witness, we ought to consider what would be most loving and not what would publicly be perceived to be most loving.

This is an uncomfortable principle, especially if one disagrees (as I do) with some of Augustine's decisions about when severity was appropriate.[26] Justifying severity in the name of love strikes me as one of a number of ways in which the rhetoric of Christian love is used to thinly disguise what amounts to cruelty. The misuse of this principle does not, in my mind, mean we should abandon it altogether. It does seem right to me—if I think of what is required of a good parent or teacher, for example—that sometimes acting in others' best-interest may earn their dislike. I believe Augustine is right that seeking others' approval or affection may hamper our ability to discern what is in their best interest. Augustine is also aware of how those in positions of authority may be inappropriately severe because they enjoy their superiority over others; what use we

---

[24]*Homilies on the First Epistle of John*, 8.9.

[25]Ibid.

[26]I am thinking in particular of how Augustine supported the treatment of the Donatists, whom he regarded as heretics who were threatening the well-being of the true church. For how Augustine's thinking on this particular use of coercion fits within his theology, the most deservedly authoritative discussion is Robert Markus, *Saeculum: History and Society in the Theology of St. Augustine* (Cambridge: Cambridge University Press, 1970), 142–143. I have found it especially helpful to consider how there are resources within Augustine's own thinking to criticize his decisions on this front. For this approach, I recommend Eric Gregory, *Politics and the Order of Love: An Augustinian Ethic of Democratic Citizenship* (Chicago: University of Chicago Press, 2010), 297–306; and John Milbank, *Theology and Social Theory: Beyond Secular Reason* (Oxford: Blackwell Publishers, 1990), 363, 390.

make of such positions, as we shall see, is an especially crucial topic in our self-examination. In other words, Augustine sees the self-deception that may be involved when we claim to act in the name of love. This would be one way to criticize some of Augustine's own thought and action on thoroughly Augustinian grounds.

A final positive result of freedom from the need for others' approval is that it facilitates love of one's enemy. Enemy love is the ultimate challenge to communicative goodness, as love is extended even to those who do not love in return; in this way, as Jesus says in the Sermon on the Mount, God's own generosity is communicated. Augustine ties enemy-love to self-criticism. In the text just quoted above, he says: "Show mercy, then, as men of merciful hearts; because in loving enemies also, you love brethren."[27] The connection between Augustine's immediately preceding discussion and this encouragement to love our enemies is not immediately evident. The underlying connection is the following: only if I act for the good of another, and not for their approval, will I be able to love my enemy. If I act for others' approval, I am only likely to act for those who will praise me. The privacy of self-criticism before God in conscience, then, is a means by which I prepare myself to love even my enemy; I gradually free myself from a constant preoccupation with others' reactions to my actions and instead orient myself according to what I discern to be their needs. We might say, then, that the private practice of self-criticism is oriented to discerning the true public good, which includes even those who may despise me.

Receiving goodness from others

A practice of solitude may also serve to make us better at recognizing what is good about others. We shift our focus from examining ourselves about how we may communicate goodness to others to instead attending to how we receive goodness from them. We first need to examine further Augustine's understanding of human equality. One key Scriptural basis for that equality is Christ's command that I am to love my neighbor "as myself." Augustine

---

[27]*Homilies on the First Epistle of John*, 8.10.

frequently explicates this with a spatial metaphor that pictures all human beings in the middle of a hierarchy. As he writes in a crucial early statement, there are four objects of love: "one, that which is above us [God]; two, that which we are [self]; three, that which is close to us [fellow human beings]; four, that which is beneath us [other, non-human creatures]."[28] This hierarchy is the way things really are and so is the basis for a discerning love: we are to love God above all else and love all human beings equally. This hierarchy also indicates that the most fundamental relation that all created things have is their relation to God. If I am to love other creatures well, then my love ought to acknowledge their relation to God as the defining feature of their creaturehood; and because of that relation, I look for how they reflect God's goodness to me. The radical implication for Augustine is that all human beings are love-able because of how they reflect God's goodness as God's creatures inevitably do: "every human being, precisely as human, is to be loved."[29]

A leading question to ask myself in solitude, then, is whether I love another human being as an equal, which is to say as a creature whose value, like my own, derives primarily from being known and loved by God. The practical application of this for our self-criticism is that we ought to interrogate ourselves about what we love when we love another person. Too often, Augustine believes, we love another based on either some need they satisfy for us or some pleasure we get from them. In *City of God*, Augustine contrasts the "freedom of judgment" with alternate subjective measures of the value of created things. He writes:

> When it comes to free exercise of judgment, evidently, the considered exercise of judgment has the advantage over the pressure of need or the satisfaction of wants. For reason considers what value a thing has in itself, as part of the way things are, whereas the logic of urgent need is that of means to ends. Reason considers what appears to be true according to the light of the mind, whereas the goal of satisfaction is that of agreeable indulgence of the bodily senses.[30]

---

[28]*Teaching Christianity*, 1.23.22.
[29]Ibid., 1.27.28.
[30]*City of God*, 11.16. My translation, with assistance from Oliver O'Donovan.

The problem arises when need or want alone are the means by which we determine the value of creatures God has made. The contrast with judgment indicates why: whereas we can judge the value a thing has as a creature within a wider horizon of its relations, including that creature's relation to God, in the case of need my relation to that creature defines my perception; whereas we judge that value by reason, in the case of want it is determined entirely by the pleasure another provides. Applied specifically to love of our fellow human beings, Augustine argues that if our love of another is entirely in terms of need or want, we do not love them as equals. Another hierarchy is at work, often where I am at the top. The opposite is also true, of course, that if another loves me entirely on the basis of some want or need I satisfy, then I may have surrendered my equality with the other.

In short, need and want narrow my perception of a fellow creature's goodness to how this person does or does not satisfy me. So Augustine says when one loves a human being on this basis one loves them "as a mule or the baths or a peacock or a parrot, that is, by way of getting some temporal enjoyment or advantage, he is bound to be enslaved not to the other person, but ... to the foul and detestable vice of not loving a human being as a human being ought to be loved."[31] The latter examples all involve reducing a human being to a piece of meat or a form of idle entertainment; our love may be responding far too partially to what is good about another. We need to look again and look better. Augustine thinks that we can slip into this kind of narrowing of our perception of another's goodness based on the roles that we play in each other's lives. In an especially difficult saying, he suggests we should not simply love another as "one's immediate family, brothers, sisters, children, wives, husbands are loved, or any other kith and kin, or one's next-door neighbors or fellow citizens." He anticipates that some may regard this as "inhuman," and he responds that the true inhumanity would be "not loving in [another] what belongs to God but loving what belongs to you."[32] The challenge is to attend to another in a way that exceeds their defined role in your life, to open yourself up to the fuller depth of their humanity, as creatures known and loved

---

[31]Augustine, *True Religion*, trans. Edmund Hill, in *On Christian Belief*, 46.87.
[32]Ibid., 46.88.

by God. In so doing, the value that my love acknowledges will not arise merely from whatever relation that person has to me.

Augustine advises that those who have a role of superiority over another ought to be especially rigorous in interrogating their love. This includes, in an example that is strikingly challenging and psychologically acute, the needy people we may assist in some way: we ought to consider whether our love for those we help may be bound up with an enjoyment of their dependence on us: "For if you have done a kindness to the wretched, perchance you desire to lift up yourself over against him ... He was in need, you bestowed; you seem to yourself greater because you bestowed, than he upon whom it was bestowed."[33] The danger of enjoying inequality lies especially in how I may be, in ways unknown to myself, not actually working to ensure that the others that I serve become equal to me. Augustine is distinguishing here between the fundamental equality that we all share, as creatures of God, and the various kinds of secondary inequality that exist between us.

One particular way to discern whether I may not love another as an equal is the presence of envy. Our self-criticism, then, ought to involve an emotional inventory, so that we might search out what our feelings toward others may reveal about our love for them. Augustine continues the theme of how we may actually desire those we serve to always remain in need of our assistance so that we may remain superior to them: "As long as he is slow, he learns from you ... therefore you seem to be the superior, because you are the teacher; he the inferior, because the learner. Except you wish him to be your equal, you wish to have him always a learner. But if you wish him always a learner, you will be an envious teacher."[34] Just as in terms of charitable giving, if I love another as an inferior, then I may be reluctant to work to overcome that inequality; so too the teacher who enjoys his superiority over his students will be an envious teacher. Undoubtedly this will hamper his ability to assist his students. Envy, in Augustine's analysis, will likely arise when we regard ourselves as fundamentally superior to others; in other words, as he puts it, "envy is the daughter of pride." Pride is

---

[33]*Homilies on the First Epistle of John*, 8.5.
[34]Ibid., 8.8.

a particularly fertile mother, he continues, because "she is unable to be barren; wherever she is, she immediately gives birth."[35]

We have thus far considered our self-criticism of why we love those we do love; a further basis for scrutinizing one's conscience is why we do not love. The most extreme case here is those with whom we have some basis for hatred, including our enemies, though what Augustine says here likely applies to all those whom we feel neutral or more generally negative about. We saw that in the Sermon on the Mount, as elsewhere, Jesus defines perfection as loving even one's enemies and thereby reflecting God's abundant generosity toward all. If we examine our loves before God in order to highlight the gap between God's seeing of another and our seeing, the most demanding work on that front is our enemy.

We saw that Augustine invites us to search out the presence of envy as a sign of distorted love; he also advises us to pay close attention to anger. He does not think that anger can be eradicated, nor does he think it should be. Feeling angry can rouse us to respond to wrongdoing or injustice, whether it is committed by ourselves or others.[36] When it comes to self-examination, though, he advises we pay close attention to whether anger may indicate a desire for vengeance.[37] Pursuing vengeance is not an option.[38] While it may be our responsibility to act when a wrong is done, Augustine believes we often let anger linger, or even tend to it and inflame it, without

---

[35]*Sermons (341–400)*, trans. Edmund Hill (New York: New City Press, 1995), 354.5.
[36]Anger with oneself may provoke confession and commitment to change; see *Confessions*, 9.4.10; *Expositions of the Psalms*, 4.6; *Sermons*, 19.2 and 113.2.2. So too anger with another may lead us to act when we should; see *Letters*, 151.7 and *City of God*, 9.5. The paradigmatic example of such just anger is parental anger. When a child has done wrong, anger may come from love and lead to correction; see *Expositions of the Psalms*, third exposition of 30.4, and *Sermons*, 82.2, 211.4, and 387.2.
[37]See *City of God*, 14.15, and *Sermons*, 58.8, 63.2, and 211.6.
[38]Augustine thinks even when the Bible seems to suggest believers should desire or pursue vengeance, these verses ought to be read otherwise. To take one example: Augustine argues that Paul's advice that we are to feed our enemy and by so doing "you will be heaping coals of fire upon his head" (Rom. 12:20) is not outlining a particularly clever strategy for revenge. Instead Paul is suggesting that by doing good to one who did me wrong I will be confronting him with his wrongdoing and thus potentially cause him to correct himself; see *Teaching Christianity*, 3.16.24; *Expositions of the Psalms*, 78.14; and *Sermons*, 149.18.19.

acknowledging it or acting to address it constructively. Noticing and addressing one's anger are crucial because of how quickly it can, Augustine thinks, "grow cold" and become hatred.[39] He argues that Scripture's advice to not let the sun set on our anger[40] intends to prevent its swift descent to hatred. And anger's destructive qualities are equally as swift: "just as vinegar spoils a container if it is kept there too long, so anger ruins a heart if it lasts until the next day."[41] Augustine connects the blindness brought about by the beam of hatred with two verses from the *Epistle of First John*: to hate our brother is not only to be in darkness[42] but to be guilty of murder[43]: "As far as you're concerned, you have killed the person you hate."[44] If we let anger fester, it amounts to a kind of removal of the other from our view. We blind ourselves to their goodness as creatures of God and so foreclose the possibility of loving them. This underlines the need for an ongoing discipline of self-interrogation in solitude. We need first to notice anger so that we can address it, rather than letting it fester and grow into hatred. Indeed, Augustine says that the presence of hatred within us, whether for a friend or an enemy, is one of the ways that our inner space of retreat will become repellent to us and we won't want to rest there with God.[45]

What would Augustine have us do, then, when in our self-examination we discover some distortion to our love or some absence of love or presence of anger or hatred toward others? A metaphor from a contemporary poet may prove useful here. Jane Hirshfield suggests that many good poems have what she refers to as a "window-moment" in which "they change their direction of gaze in a way that suddenly opens a broadened landscape of meaning and feeling. Encountering such a moment, the reader breathes in

---

[39]*Expositions of the Psalms*, third exposition of 30.4; *Sermons*, 49.7.7, 58.7.8, and 82.1.1. Augustine sees Jesus in the Sermon on the Mount outlining the relation between anger and hatred in his image of the "beam" in one's eye; see Luc Verheijen, "The Straw, the Beam, the Tusculan Disputations and the Rule of Saint Augustine—On a Surprising Augustinian Exegesis," *Augustinian Studies*, no. 2 (1971): 17–36.
[40]Eph. 4:26.
[41]*Letters (156–210)*, trans. Roland Teske (New York: New City Press, 2004), 210.2.
[42]*Expositions of the Psalms*, 30–3.4.
[43]*Sermons*, 49.7.7, 58.7.8, and 387.2.
[44]*Sermons*, 58.7.8.
[45]*Expositions of the Psalms*, second exposition of 33.8.

some new infusion, as steeply perceptible as any physical window's increase of light, scent, sound, or air."[46] Hirshfield's metaphor is not the first time we have encountered windows. As we discussed in the first chapter, in *Middlemarch* Dorothea's self-examination in solitude eventually led her to look out the window and see others more clearly. The image of the window, then, connects how time in solitude can improve our ability to see both ourselves and others more clearly. I want to apply Hirshfield's concept of "window-moments" to consider how Augustine understands the role of faith in our self-interrogation. Augustine believes that faith itself may offer a "window-moment" as the believer subordinates her seeing of another to God's seeing of that other. It's not that our seeing and God's seeing can ever wholly coincide; yet Augustine does believe that the gifts of faith, hope, and love serve to give us glimmers of what God sees when we look at others.

To help us see how faith can facilitate such "window-moments," I will intersperse our discussion of Augustine with another literary case study, Marilynne Robinson's novel *Gilead*. The narrator, an elderly minister, John Ames, sets out to write a letter that he hopes his son will read when he is an adult. As an old man in poor health, Ames expects that his young son will grow up largely without his father. The letter is an attempt to set down in words what he thinks his son should know about his family history and some essentials of the Christian faith. As well, the letter is, as all letters are, a work of solitude, in this case solitude in God's company. Ames tells us that, as one who is accustomed to writing prayers and sermons, and as a man of constant prayer, "writing has always felt like praying ... You feel that you are with someone. I feel I am with you now."[47] The "you" in the latter sentence is his son, whom he imagines reading this years later. Equally, though, his letter also involves him praying for his son and so he writes before God too. Elsewhere Ames describes even "the most private thought" as involving three persons: "the self that yields the thought, the self that acknowledges and in some way responds to the thought, and the Lord. That is a

[46]Jane Hirshfield, *Ten Windows: How Great Poems Transform the World* (New York: Alfred A. Knopf, 2015), 151.
[47]Marilynne Robinson, *Gilead* (New York: Farrar, Straus and Giroux, 2004), 19.

remarkable thing to consider."[48] This letter, then, is the culmination of Ames's lifetime of prayer and writing with and before God.

The subject of Ames's letter gradually changes from its intended topic of history and instruction to his struggles to know how to deal with—and love—the return of his best friend's son, Jack Ames Boughton, who was not only named after him but baptized by him too. The latter were both gestures intended to convey that Jack was entrusted to Ames as his own son, as he was then childless, having lost his first wife and baby daughter. Ames devoted a great deal of time in the first part of the letter to relations between fathers and sons, particularly the relation between his grandfather and father, as well as his own relationship with his father. At several points, Ames is upset that the letter seems to have been hijacked by his agonizing about Jack. The change of topic is superficial; fundamentally, the relation between Ames and Jack is another story of a fraught relationship with father and son, marked especially by Ames struggle to love Jack.

As we shall see, Ames's hostility toward Jack depends, at least in part, on how conclusions about Jack's character have gradually taken on the status of facts. For Augustine, considering God's seeing of others may serve to remind us how limited our perception of others is. In particular, Augustine argues the conclusions we make about others' intentions are often guesswork, yet that guesswork dramatically influences our sense of others. One interpretation Augustine has of Jesus's command to "Judge not" is that we are to restrain ourselves from speculating about others' motives.[49] Often what we see admits of various interpretations; we regularly cannot accurately conclude what lies behind an action, and yet how many of our judgments are based on such interpretive leaps? Because "every heart is shut against each other"[50] we can only judge on the basis of "what is out in the open," whereas judging the heart is "God's privilege."[51] Thus, "Judge not" alerts us to all those actions

---

[48]Ibid., 45.

[49]See Augustine, *The Lord's Sermon on the Mount*, 2.18.59; *Expositions of the Psalms*, twelfth exposition of 118.4; *The Christian Combat*, trans. Robert P. Russell in *Writings of Saint Augustine* (New York: CIMA Publishing, 1947), 27.29.

[50]*Expositions of the Psalms*, 55.9.

[51]*Sermons (230-272B)*, trans. Edmund Hill (New York: New City Press, 1993), 243.5.

in which another's intention is either unknowable or ambiguous. We are to assume that the intention is good and leave the judgment to God.[52] Augustine still concedes that we may be required to make judgments about others' motives when we are unsure, as in the case of civil judge. Still he thinks that we often needlessly engage in speculation about others' motives that taints our perception of them. To subordinate our seeing to God's seeing is not only a matter of exercising some humility when interpreting others' motives; such humility about our knowledge does not require faith. What faith in God adds is the possibility of entrusting others' unknowability to God.

In *Gilead*, Ames gradually comes to question the motives that he attributed to Jack. He does so by returning to some of his earliest memories of Jack and considering the interpretations of Jack's character and motives that are lurking there, often unacknowledged; the novel expertly represents how we often take our interpretations of what happened as factual. Ames believes that remembering can be inspired by God. He writes, "Perhaps this is the one thing I wish to tell you. Sometimes the visionary aspect of any particular day comes to you in the memory of it, or it opens to you over time ... I believe there are visions that come to us only in memory, in retrospect."[53] This claim prepares us as readers to see what Ames learns about Jack by returning to his memories of him. Reviewing some of Jack's wrongs, one of which is especially glaring and tragic, in his first recollection of it Ames can only see cruelty in Jack. This act of remembering confirms his antipathy toward Jack. Later in the letter, having reread a section he just wrote, he writes, "I noticed I have said [Jack] seemed lonely. That was one very strange thing about him."[54] What first appears as a passing comment gradually becomes the basis for reconsidering Ames's perceptions of Jack. Thus, Ames records how it was not only remembering Jack's loneliness that made a difference; he also reviewed his account of the memory, which causes him to revise his perception of Jack's meanness. Given that Jack belonged to such a loving and large family, Ames cannot make sense of Jack's loneliness. Ames's very

---

[52]Augustine, *The Lord's Sermon on the Mount*, 1.18.59–60.
[53]Robinson, *Gilead*, 91.
[54]Ibid., 183.

inability to make sense of Jack is already itself an altering of his perception of him. At one point he writes, "My point is that he was always a mystery."[55] This altering of Ames's perceptions of Jack enacts Augustine's interpretation to "Judge not"; Ames changes from having a firm conclusion about Jack's character to acknowledging that Jack vastly exceeds Ames's understanding.

For both Augustine and Ames, faith in God's seeing of others may serve to inspire a renewed looking at others to yield much-needed "window-moments." One such window-moment is the change of perspective that may come when we regard another as constantly subject to God's creative work. One way Augustine highlighted this activity was by distinguishing how each person of the Trinity is inseparably involved in the life of every particular creature. In one of his earliest discussions of this view, he explicates it in terms of three analytical questions that were taught in classical education: "Whether a thing exists at all, whether it is this or something else, and whether it should be approved or disapproved?"[56] These questions gradually familiarize us with whatever object we are considering, as we first establish whether it even exists, then what its particular nature is, and finally come to some evaluation of that object as it expresses its nature.[57] Augustine establishes an analogy between each of these questions and the nature and work of each Trinitarian person: the Father, as the Source within the relations between the divine persons, grants existence; the Son, as the One through whom all things were created and re-created, gives them their nature; and the Holy Spirit, as divine love, unites all things to God and so both maintains their existence and causes them to flourish.

To also see an example of this from a later work, we see these same three questions of classical education reappear in *City of God*

---

[55]Ibid., 184.

[56]Augustine, *Miscellany of Eighty-Three Questions*, 18. I have amended the translation slightly. For the last question, I have chosen "approved or disapproved" to translate "approbandum improbandumve," in contrast to Ramsay's rendering of "appropriate or inappropriate"; the latter phrase seems too narrow to me to capture the breadth of judgments I think Augustine has in mind.

[57]According to Lewis Ayres, Augustine's appropriation of these questions for theological purposes was unprecedented in the Latin Christian tradition; see his *Augustine and the Trinity* (Cambridge: Cambridge University Press, 2010), 66.

when Augustine outlines how all three persons of the Trinity are implicitly present in the description of God's creation in Genesis[58]:

> Who made it? By what means did He make it? and Why did He make it? For the Father of the Word is understood to be the one who said, 'Let it be made.' And what was made when he said this was undoubtedly made by his Word. And when it says, *God saw that it was good*, it signifies clearly that God did not make what he made out of any necessity, or out of any need for something useful to himself, but simply out of sheer goodness; that is, he made what he made because it is good. This is said after the thing had been made, rather than before, precisely in order to indicate that the thing made does, in fact, correspond to the goodness on account of which it was made. And if this goodness is rightly understood to be the Holy Spirit, then the whole Trinity is intimated to us in its works.[59]

Augustine's emphasis that God did not create for God's own sake recalls our discussion of how personal want or need can narrow one's perception of another's goodness. To attend to another as constantly subject to God's ongoing creative activity is to expect to find goodness in another that is not circumscribed by our particular relation to her or him. As well, the inseparable creative activity of the Trinity as described here may attune one to the dynamic and diverse ways that God's work may be visible on another.

In short, then, faith in the Triune God can inform our perception of others. For one thing, Augustine argues, as all our fellow human beings are given their human nature through the Son, we should expect to find something good about even the person we currently hate. If we are finding someone difficult to love, then we might look for what we share with them as a result of our shared humanity. This process of discovery involves situating what we may justifiably find is reprehensible about another within the larger context of their creatureliness: "This is precisely the principle we maintain, that we should hate our enemy for what is evil in him, that is, for wickedness;

---

[58]For other similar examples, see also *On True Religion*, 12.24 and 55.112–113; and *The Literal Meaning of Genesis*, 1.5.11.
[59]*City of God*, 11.24.

while we also love our enemy for that which is good in him, that is, for his nature as a social and rational being."[60] Attending to signs of another's social or rational nature likely expands drastically what we observe in another, given that so often hatred or dislike may arise from an exclusive focus on only one aspect of another. To judge others entirely in terms of their sin, as Augustine warns professional judges, is to deny they are fellow creatures: "You came from the same workshop, from the hands of the same craftsman; the same clay provided your raw material."[61] To fail to look for the goodness that comes with our shared humanity, in other words, is to deny the nature that we hold in common, as given from God.

Thus, to return to Ames and Jack, throughout *Gilead* Ames demonstrates a remarkable sensitivity toward perceiving God's goodness everywhere. Ames, to choose only one example, delights in the basic properties of water.[62] And repeatedly tells us that, as a man of faith, he believes, "existence is the essential thing and the holy thing."[63] Like Augustine, then, Ames believes that all of God's creatures, in their very being, ought to reflect some quality of God's goodness. Eventually, though it takes much work, Ames sees this goodness in Jack too. His acknowledgment that Jack is a mystery, discussed above, is a temporary step, a clearing away of hardened perceptions of Jack, which will eventually free him up to see Jack's goodness. By the conclusion of the novel, Jack has revealed to John why he came home, which serves to further alter Ames's perception of Jack, both past and present. Ames relays the details of it in his letter, and then, by way of justifying why he would share so much intimate detail of another person's life, he writes, "I just don't know another way to let you see the beauty there is in him."[64] Ames now feels a responsibility to help others to see the goodness that is present in Jack.

What if, unlike Ames, we have Jacks in our own lives and we find it impossible to spot anything good about them? Augustine advises

---

[60]*Answer to Faustus, a Manichean*, trans. Roland Teske (New York: New City Press, 2007), 19.24.
[61]*Sermons (1–19)*, 13.8.
[62]Robinson, *Gilead*, 27–28.
[63]Ibid., 190.
[64]Ibid., 232.

us that we should, at the very least, not give up hope that goodness might be evident in them someday. Our attention, in such cases, can turn instead to how they are works-in-progress, like we are. In terms of the creative activity of the Trinity, this corresponds to the work of the Holy Spirit, who holds us in being and reforms us to better reflect God's goodness. Attention to how the Spirit might be at work in another attunes us to their potential, thus opening up a focus for our love in the absence of anything else. Our love, then, as he writes in a letter, responds to the unrealized potential in another: "we should love those who are bad in order that they might cease to be bad, just as we love the ill not in order that they may remain ill but in order that they may be healed."[65] In short, others can change. Another interpretation Augustine offers of Christ's "Judge not," then, is to point out that even if we are confident that another has committed wrong, we don't know how, by the grace of God, another may change. We must never let our judgments harden into final conclusions about another; to "Judge not" includes holding all judgments we have made as provisional.[66]

Even recognizing that we ourselves are temporal creatures who are inevitably works-in-progress can at least alter the tenor, if not the content, of our perceptions of others. The most transformative way to acknowledge that we are all works-in-progress is to constantly recognize our own need for forgiveness. We will be forced to do so, Augustine thinks, if we pray the Lord's Prayer every day, especially the petition: "And forgive us our debts, as we also have forgiven our debtors." In this verse, Augustine sees Jesus binding together our receiving forgiveness from God with our offering it to others; to request forgiveness from God without granting it to others contradicts this. Augustine refers to this verse as the "terms,"[67] "condition,"[68] "rule,"[69] "bargain,"[70] even the "instrument, read out in court" of our forgiveness.[71] He assumes that this prayer will be

---

[65]*Letters*, 153.5.14.
[66]Augustine, *The Lord's Sermon on the Mount*, 2.18.61; *Letters*, 130.2.4; and *The Christian Combat*, 27.29.
[67]*Expositions of the Psalms*, 143.8, and *Sermons*, 114.5.
[68]*Expositions of the Psalms*, 143.7.
[69]*Sermons (51–94)*, 83.2.2.
[70]*Sermons (94A-147A)*, trans. Edmund Hill (New York: New City Press, 1992), 114.5.
[71]Ibid.

a daily part of a Christian's practice of solitude. Augustine thinks that these words may serve to provoke self-examination "inside in your hearts, and find that you ought not to have done what you did, ought not to have said what you did; beg pardon, brothers and sisters, from your brothers and sisters."[72] We must also, Augustine thinks, be vigilant in offering others forgiveness if we can pray these words "without any anxiety or worry, and not to stumble or stammer or grow dumb under the prickings of conscience."[73] This includes, to his mind, a self-examination of one's own shortcomings that will increase one's readiness to be forgiving of others either because you identify things you have done wrong and ask for God's mercy[74] or because you also recognize that your self-examination is not accurate or comprehensive; either way, your sensitivity to your own reliance on God's mercy, heightened by the examination of one's conscience in solitude, should serve to make you more ready to forgive.

Augustine even thinks that there is an inner practice of forgiveness that we should engage in constantly. He bases this suggestion on Jesus's teaching in the Sermon on the Mount that alms should be given not for others' approval but for God's approval. Augustine writes that almsgiving can be done "in your conscience itself ... even if [you] lack money or whatever else could be given to the needy."[75] He refers to there being two kinds of charitable deeds to do to another,[76] either giving or forgiving.[77] The latter, he emphasizes, can be done anytime and anywhere, and does not depend on having any material wealth to share. In this way, that private inner room becomes a place of reconciliation. To call before our minds the imagined presence of others, and to evaluate our feelings toward and treatment of them, is one way to follow Jesus's instruction to give alms before God who sees in secret. This does not deny, of course, the need for outward engagement with others, whatever the

---

[72]*Sermons (184-229Z)*, trans. Edmund Hill (New York: New City Press, 1993), 211.3.
[73]Ibid., 208.2.
[74]*Letters*, 140.31.75.
[75]Augustine, *The Lord's Sermon on the Mount*, 2.2,9.
[76]*Letters*, 157.2.10; *Sermons*, 42.1 and 114.5.
[77]These two are suggested by their pairing in these words of Jesus: "Forgive and you will be forgiven; give and it will be given to you ... for the measure you give will be the measure you get back" (Lk. 6:37–38).

case may be. Instead, Augustine thinks an ongoing process of self-examination, which will involve identifying those toward whom we feel some measure of anger or hatred, is a means to prepare us to continue to communicate God's goodness in our public lives.

As well, it is an acknowledgment of our fundamental equality under God; just as others are in need of forgiveness, so too am I. To return one last time to *Gilead*, at one point Ames dismisses his need to forgive Jack and asserts that his remembering Jack's childhood and teenage years has nothing to do with forgiving him: "remembering and forgiving can be contrary things. No doubt they usually are. It is not for me to forgive Jack Boughton."[78] Yet the unfolding of the novel disproves this. By returning to his memories of Jack, and interrogating his interpretations of Jack's character and motives, Ames eventually does alter his perception of Jack in a way that amounts to forgiveness. In one especially telling detail, before he leaves again, Ames gives to Jack an old copy of Feuerbach's *Essence of Christianity*, which Ames's brother Edward had given to him years ago. While Ames has reconciled himself to how Jack is a son to him, this passing on of a gift he received from his brother to Jack also indicates a certain new fraternal relationship between them. In coming to a wider recognition of Jack's goodness, Ames can also acknowledge their equality as siblings under God.[79]

Conclusion

The primary purpose of this chapter was to demonstrate how Christian solitude is not antisocial. Instead, the privacy of conscience supports the publicity of love. To regard oneself as a mediator of God's goodness involves both attending to what one's reputation may communicate to others and being willing to tarnish or altogether sacrifice one's reputation if that is what love of another as an equal demands. As well, we also saw that an ongoing examination of our perceptions of, and actions toward, others may serve to heighten our sensitivity toward their goodness

---

[78]Robinson, *Gilead*, 164.
[79]Ibid., 164.

and how we share in our incomplete status as creatures in constant need of forgiveness. Augustine's idiosyncratic application of God's Triune creative activity on others offers one "window" by which we might look again at others and see them differently. We saw another Christian expression of this renewal of sight in *Gilead*. In short, Augustine's Christian practice of solitude is a work of love, committed to loving others, including one's enemies, as equals under God. In this way, I suggest, Augustine marks himself as an especially able and effective interpreter of Jesus's teaching on solitude.

4

The Flight from Solitude

*Do not love the world or the things in the world. The love
of the Father is not in those who love the world; for all that
is in the world—the lust of the flesh, lust of the eyes, and
pride of life—comes not from the Father but from the world.*

—1 JOHN 2:15-16

In the two preceding chapters, we saw that Augustine recommends a practice of solitude in which we retreat from others' company and engage in conversation with and before God in the privacy of our conscience. By pursuing God's company in solitude, we may gain an alternative perspective on ourselves and others. Let me repeat a number of qualifications to this account: first, this is only one type of solitude; second, solitude is not the only means of pursuing God's companionship; and, third, it is not the only means of sharpening our capacity for self-criticism or helping us to love others better. Yet in the constant company of others, Augustine thinks, we may not have an opportunity to critically examine ourselves and our relationships with others, both how they influence us and how we love them. With Augustine's account of the moral necessity of solitude in mind, we may now return to a question we explored at the very beginning of this inquiry regarding the contemporary threat to solitude. In the Introduction, we considered various thinkers' analyses of why solitude is especially under threat in our own day due to unprecedented technological developments and distinct cultural influences. These are particular barriers to finding solitude in the twenty-first century. Another factor inhibiting the practice of solitude belongs to a more perennial source, our desire as social creatures for the good of human companionship or, to put this negatively, our fear of the evil of loneliness. Augustine affirms our social nature as given by God and regards our flourishing in this life and our perfection in the next life as dependent on human community. Yet Augustine does not think that our social nature alone explains why we may neglect or avoid solitude. A further answer he offers to this question is sin, specifically the sin of pride, which he defines as love of one's own power.

How does Augustine's definition of pride relate to our flight from solitude? Love of one's own power impedes self-examination in solitude in two ways: first, this love keeps us constantly busy acting outwardly in the world, so that we can experience our own power, and by so doing we rarely carve out time to pause and turn within to examine ourselves. Further, as we shall see, a consequence of this busyness is that our roomy inner space becomes cluttered and so inhospitable to dwelling alone with God. Second, even if we take a break from our busyness, love of our own power tends to have us resist self-criticism, especially self-criticism that relies on acknowledging our need for other companions to help us to know ourselves. In the first chapter, I distinguished different companions in solitude, whose company offers a different way of seeing ourselves. Even as we may seek solitude to gain some independence from others' perspectives, we can only do so through dependence on other influences. This point is especially obvious in the second and third kinds of solitude, in which we rely on the influence of nature or God to help our self-examination. Even the first kind of solitude, in which we seek our own companionship, involves the recognition that we are always incomplete, in need of alternating between time alone and time with others in order that we are not idly swept away by some destructive or stultifying consensus.

Based on the biblical verses cited above, Augustine believes there are three forms of busyness that we turn to out of love of our own power: lust of the flesh, lust of the eyes, and pride of life; each is a distorted love that expresses itself in pursuit of one of the following: physical pleasure, stimulation, or domination over others. With the first, in our desire for physical pleasure we act as consumers who regard the world as little more than a means to satisfy our thirsts. The second refers to a desire for stimulation, not necessarily of the pleasurable variety, and often seemingly intellectual. The final kind of busyness, by far the most destructive, is a desire for domination over others. With each of these kinds of busyness, out of love for our own power we dominate creation in some way in order that we can affirm our mastery over it, and so we refuse to recognize any limits to our busyness other than the authority of our own desire. In particular, each form of busyness prevents us from turning within to engage in dialogue with and before God.

The beginning of pride

We begin with what Augustine regards as the beginning of human pride, namely how Adam and Eve's eating of the fruit reflects love of one's own power. When interpreted historically, the story of Adam and Eve's snack describes how these first humans, created good by God, deprive themselves and their descendants of that goodness by rejecting their dependence on God; when interpreted allegorically, the story discloses how each one of us repeats that same fateful decision in our lives. In this instance, Augustine's belief that the story happened historically is the grounds for also reading it allegorically; we see in Adam and Eve the origin of a human propensity that we inherit from them. So we can, I think, disagree with Augustine about the historical accuracy of those opening chapters of Genesis (as I do) and still find his analysis of the story yields genuine insights into human nature.

Adam and Eve's eating of the fruit is a delusional assertion of their independence, acting as though they can define who they are and what they should do apart from their relation to God, their Creator. Eve did not want to know and act in accordance with, and dependence on, God's intention for her, instead she wanted to strike out on her own. And Adam made a similar decision to disregard his dependence on God when he followed Eve's lead. Augustine characterizes their decision thus: "the soul, loving its own power, slides away from the whole which is common to all into the part which is its own private property."[1] Another way he articulates their decision is as a "perverse kind of elevation" in which Adam and Eve abandon God as their "foundation" in order to "become and

---

[1] *The Trinity*, trans. Edmund Hill (New York: New City Press, 1991), 12.3.14.

remain one's own foundation."[2] We see, then, that pride involves the rejection of relationship, first and foremost our relation of dependence on God, but, following from that, the rejection of other relationships too. So it is not an accident, in Augustine's reading, that soon after eating the fruit, Adam and Eve start blaming others instead of taking responsibility for their wrongdoing. They reject their need for forgiveness and healing after they have done wrong by attempting to unload responsibility on to others.[3]

Adam and Eve's choice of independence from God has disastrous consequences. One example is Adam and Eve's shame at their nakedness. In Augustine's analysis, when they see themselves as beloved creatures of God, they see their given naked bodies as beautiful, and so they don't feel any need to cover themselves up. The only piece of "clothing" they care about is that they are images of God, what Augustine calls their "garment of grace."[4] So their original nakedness shows their "simplicity" and their complete lack of "pretense."[5] Such simplicity is the basis for effortless companionship with each other and with God.

By contrast, when Adam and Eve clothe themselves with the fig leaves, they put human artistry at the service of appearing good. Augustine finds much to inspire his imagination with the description of Adam and Eve's sewing fig leaves together to cover themselves. In one commentary, Augustine says that they reject their given simplicity to become fashioners of "fraudulent pretenses."[6] Adam and Eve begin the long history of using appearance to hide or disguise reality, as the fig leaves cover their genitals.[7] Out of their shame they want to "conceal" their simplicity.[8] Augustine notes that fig leaves would likely have proven itchy and that feature of their

---

[2]*City of God*, trans. R. W. Dyson, 14.13. I have opted for Dyson's translation here because his rendering of "principio/principium" as "foundation" strikes me as more appropriate to the sense of the passage (including the spatial metaphors at work in it) than Babcock's choice of "principle."

[3]*On Genesis: A Refutation of the Manichees*, trans. Edmund Hill, in *On Genesis* (New York: New City Press, 2002), 2.17.25.

[4]*City of God*, 14.17.

[5]*On Genesis: A Refutation of the Manichees*, 2.16.24.

[6]Ibid., 2.15.22.

[7]Ibid.

[8]Ibid., 2.15.23.

new duds reflects a continued desire to cover over the truth with further dissembling.[9] This dissembling includes the use of language as Augustine writes that "they sew together fine words without the fruit of good works, in order while living badly to cover up their baseness by speaking well."[10] Their clothing, in short, represents a turn to performative goodness, the very posturing that Augustine believes Jesus criticized as hypocrisy.

This focus on clothing also reflects another feature of Augustine's analysis of Adam and Eve's sin: how their lives are now centered on their bodies as their private property. As Augustine writes, when a soul chooses independence for itself over dependence on God, then it "tries to do its own thing … [and it does so] by its own body, which is the only part it has part-ownership in."[11] When Adam and Eve turn from their dependence on God and God's goodness, which all share as an infinite resource, they are left instead to define themselves in terms of what they can claim belongs exclusively to them: their bodies. Then, with one's body as the primary reference by which one discerns and secures value, a person "refers all its business to one or other of the following ends: curiosity, searching for bodily and temporal experience through the senses; swollen conceit, affecting to be above other souls which are given over to the senses; or carnal pleasure, plunging itself in this muddy whirlpool."[12] This description refers to the triad of sins contained in 1 John 2:15-16, quoted at the beginning of this chapter, which the author refers to as "love of the world." These are the three kinds of busyness that occupy us when we reject our dependence on God: with curiosity, we seek constant stimulation; with pride, we seek to dominate others; and with carnal pleasure, we seek to enjoy bodily sensation. When our outer life in the world is the primary way we establish and recognize value, we depend on our own actions and the reactions we receive from those actions to do so. One consequence of this is that we put the priority on acting in the world; there is, of course, much to be done, and action in the world is crucial to the vocation of human beings, placed in the garden to tend it and care for it. Even so, Augustine diagnoses constant activity, and the

---

[9]Ibid.
[10]*The Trinity*, 12.3.13.
[11]Ibid., 12.9.14.
[12]Ibid.

forms it can take, as a distorted love of power; constant activity secures our sense of self by showing to ourselves and others that we are doers who can make a difference in the world. A practice of solitude in which we pause from such activity would feel, then, like it threatens the very basis of our self-esteem.

Love of the world

Before considering each form of busyness in turn, and how it prevents us from pursuing solitude, we first need to address how peculiar, even troubling, it is that the *First Epistle of John* classifies "love of the world" as a sin. How did Augustine interpret this? One helpful answer he offers comes by an analogy. Imagine, he says, a bride who loves her wedding ring more than the groom who gave it to her. While the ring may be admirable for all sorts of reasons— its beauty, its craftsmanship, its cost—Augustine suggests that we would all think the bride mistaken, perhaps even mentally unwell, if she treasures her ring more than the person who gave it to her. The ring, after all, is a sign of the groom's commitment to his wife, and therefore its ultimate value comes from their relationship to each other. If the groom did a good job choosing a ring, its qualities may also serve to communicate his love for her. It is not, then, that she can't love the ring, but she must love it in a way that also acknowledges its significance within the context of their marriage. He drives home his point:

> If the bride said, 'This ring is enough for me. Now I don't want to see his face again', what sort of person would she be? Who wouldn't detest this crazy woman? Who wouldn't convict her of an adulterous mind? You love gold instead of the man, you love a ring instead of your bridegroom ... A bridegroom gives a pledge for the very purpose that he himself may be loved in his pledge. That is why God gave you these things, then; love God who made them. There is more that God wants to give you—that is, God-self, who made them.[13]

---

[13]*Homilies on the First Epistle of John*, trans. Boniface Ramsey (New York: New City Press, 2008), 2.11.

Augustine makes evident the theological force of the analogy. If creation is made good by God and is shared with us, then it is a gift to us; to love it as a gift is to admire it and delight in it and care for it as the work of God, and so whatever love we have for the gift is secondary to the love we have for the Giver. All our relationships within creation, in other words, derive from God, who is the origin and sustainer of creation. All our relationships to creatures, then, must somehow acknowledge our and their relationship to God. When the bride receives the ring as a gift from her groom, as a sign of his love, then her deliberating about the value of the ring is subordinated to her beholding of the groom's generosity.

Love of the world is a sin, then, when we love what is in the world apart from God, the ring separate from the groom who gave it to us. Most often, to Augustine's mind, this involves *over*valuing ourselves and *under*valuing those with whom we are in relationship, namely God, fellow human beings, and the rest of creation; we saw some of the ways we can undervalue others in the previous chapter. Augustine is also alive to the possibility that we may undervalue ourselves too, though he seems to regard this as a less frequent occurrence. The same problem underlies both overvaluing myself and undervaluing myself: I do not ground my sense of self in the nonnegotiable value that I have as a creature known and loved by God but think that my value depends on me or others. The result of all of this is that rather than discovering the value of myself and all other creatures as they belong to God's creation, I must somehow find another foundation for their value, often my own action in the world, and what need or pleasure, physical or psychological, various creatures satisfy for me.[14]

---

[14]It is also worth noting that there was not a prior tradition of commentary on 1 John 2:15-16 that Augustine is responding to or building on. According to Dideberg's count, the triad appears only once in Ambrose, Ambrosiaster, and Tertullian, twice in Jerome, and six times in Cyprian; see D. Dideberg, *Saint Augustin et la première epitre de saint Jean* (Paris: Editions Beauchesne, 1975), 185. In other words, Augustine's focus on this verse is unprecedented compared to earlier Latin Christian authors. His attraction to this text fits with a central concern of Augustine's career as a scholar, teacher, and preacher: to understand and communicate how we are to love God and neighbor; 1 John 15-16 clarifies the latter by identifying the opposite. Further, it also provides a kind of classification of sin that no doubt would have appealed to Augustine's desire for comprehensive understanding.

Lust of the flesh: Desire for pleasure

We come to our first form of busyness, lust of the flesh, in which we pursue sensual pleasure as the primary good. Augustine does not deny that our senses are an essential feature of our embodied nature and that physical pleasure is a God-given good. Lust of the flesh, however, is a distorted love of physical pleasure. With this lust, we regard ourselves primarily as consumers, who experience our own power by manipulating creation to satisfy us in some way or other. One indication that our pursuit of pleasure is sinful, according to Augustine, is if it does not recognize any given limits, such as what promotes health for our bodies or other creatures. The dual consequence of such a pursuit is, first, that we are occupied with external goods and so rarely turn inward for self-examination in solitude; and, second, we do not use the naturally given limits to our desire as grounds for self-examination.

When examining his own relation to food, Augustine outlines how desire for bodily pleasure often either does not notice or refuses to acknowledge any limit outside of the desire itself. While food and drink are necessary for us to maintain our health, much of our eating and drinking goes well beyond meeting that necessity. In analyzing his own relation to food and drink, Augustine locates the problem in terms of how he judges whether he has eaten enough. In theory, he should generally stop eating when he has had enough to keep his body healthy. In practice, though, Augustine says it can be difficult to know exactly how much is the right amount for health, and, further, he confesses that often he uses the justification of health to eat more than could possibly be healthy. As he writes: "what suffices to maintain health appears meager to appetite."[15] The two pleasures Augustine identifies in eating—the pleasure of the tastes themselves and the further pleasure that comes when desire begins to be sated—make it difficult to recognize what the right amount of food is for him. There is a gap, often a chasm, between how much is enough for health as opposed to pleasure. Thus Augustine surrenders to eating too much when he either does not recognize the line or when he does and blows right past it.

---

[15] *Confessions*, trans. Maria Boulding (New York: New City Press, 2007), 10. 31. 44.

Many readers—including more than a few students with whom I have read this text—have balked at what they regard as Augustine's excessive severity with himself here. The most trenchant criticism, to my mind, is that such severity may make it even more difficult to develop a healthy relationship to food by fostering obsessiveness and anxiety over portion size. Augustine does recognize that abstemiousness is as much a form of immoderation as excessiveness, though he seems to think that he, and most of us, may be guilty more of excess. I do think Augustine has accurately identified a danger. If sensual pleasure is our primary pursuit, then we often either downplay, ignore, or dismiss any limits to the pursuit of pleasure other than the (temporary) satisfaction of our desire or the end of our supply. To consider the health of my body when deciding how much to eat involves an acknowledgment that there are limits that are given to me as an embodied creature. Further, while Augustine does not address this, there is also the moral issue of the consequences of our eating habits for the health of other creatures and creation as a whole. To take these consequences into account when eating would be another way to recognize that there are given limits to my desire because I am a creature who is in relationship to other creatures and to creation. Our failure to attend to or acknowledge such limits shows how the love of the world often fails to address the realities of the world. Thus, it is not only that lust of the flesh keeps one busy with what is outward and thus prevents the turn inward to an examination of conscience alone before God; it is further that lust of the flesh prevents one from acknowledging nature as having limits that should make a moral claim on one's actions. Thoreau's example from the first chapter will be instructive here: the companionship of nature in solitude changes Thoreau because he attends to nature as having its own integrity, which educates him about what it means to be a creature alongside other creatures. By contrast, lust of the flesh attends to nature as though its primary meaning lies in whatever satisfies the consumer's desire.

Lust of the flesh: Desire for stimulation

The second kind of busyness that avoids solitude is curiosity, which corresponds to lust of the eyes. Augustine explains his association of curiosity with lust of the eyes by claiming that eyes are the most rational sense; this is evident from the frequent associations we make between seeing and knowledge (like "seeing the point").[16] Our first reaction may be to acknowledge that curiosity certainly keeps us busy, but it does not deserve to be classified as a sin because the desire for knowledge is good. Augustine, as I hope is abundantly clear by this point, was no intellectual slouch, and his pursuit of knowledge was broad and deep. But curiosity, as he defines it, is not primarily about learning; instead, he calls it "greed to experience [our] own power."[17] Curiosity is a consequence of pride, in other words, because when I am greedy to experience my own power, the learning I pursue is determined first and foremost by a desire for my stimulation. Again with this type of sin, then, the individual does not acknowledge any limit to the desire for knowledge outside of what stimulates him. The reward of curiosity comes not from bodily pleasure, as with lust of the flesh, because when pursuing lust of the eyes often what we feel is not straightforwardly pleasurable. If we think, for example, about the range of emotions that come from watching a violent movie, even if we might want to say we enjoyed feeling terrified, that enjoyment is distinguishable from the pleasure we take in eating our favorite food. Curiosity, in other words, is more indiscriminate in seeking stimulation; even though it is not straightforwardly pleasurable, somehow the intensity of the experience is desirable.

Augustine provides his friend Alypius as an example of a curious person. Augustine tells in *Confessions* of how Alypius had stopped going to Roman gladiatorial shows because he agreed with Augustine that they were immoral; years later, under the pressure of some friends, Alypius returns. He intended to go and close his eyes, but the roar of the crowd piques his interest and then "overwhelmed by curiosity," he took it all in: "As he saw the blood he gulped the brutality along with it; he did not turn away but fixed his gaze there and drank in the frenzy, not aware of what he was doing, reveling in the wicked contest and intoxicated on the sanguinary pleasure."[18] The verbs in this quotation are especially revealing.

---

[16]*Confessions*, 10.35.54.
[17]*The Trinity*, 12.11.16. Curiosity is not named here, but the triad in this passage implicitly corresponds to the triad earlier in 12.11.15, where curiosity is named.
[18]*Confessions*, 6.8.13.

Augustine implicitly compares Alypius's watching of the fight with drinking an intoxicating beverage: first, by viewing the violence it is as though he "gulped the brutality"; second, by continuing to watch the crowd he "drank in the frenzy." The ultimate result of all this drinking is that Alypius is drunk. As was the case with lust of the flesh, then, in which Augustine lamented how often when eating he crossed the line from moderation to excess, so here Alypius's viewing of the gladiatorial contest goes too far and he loses control.

If lust of the flesh threatens our bodily health (among other things), what about lust of the eyes? In Alypius's case, the men in the gladiatorial contest suffer physical and psychological hurt to entertain the crowd. The high cost of this entertainment surely makes it morally questionable. Yet, based on this description, and the larger context of this section of *Confessions*, Augustine seems far more interested in why Alypius is so taken with this fight and what effects it has on him. In *The Trinity*, Augustine offers a definition of curiosity that helps to make sense of Alypius: the curious person is "carried away by the mere love of knowing unknown things for no known reason."[19] The "no known reason" refers to how the curious person pursues knowledge that does not serve any good other than the self's stimulation; and, when stimulation in and of itself becomes the primary goal of knowledge, then the knower does not acknowledge any limits to what he should try to find out. In Alypius's case, he enjoys seeing men fight and bleed and also seeing others enjoy those same sights. While there may be good reasons to learn about and even witness such things, Alypius is not there with any such good in mind. Thus Alypius's curiosity feeds off the denigration of others, both the fighters in the ring and the audience who is watching it, who should be loved as creatures made in the image of God; as well, he is contributing to his own denigration, as he is taking those images into himself. Augustine continues in *The Trinity* to say that the curios person "hates the unknown, since he would like nothing to be unknown and everything known."[20] Augustine is not criticizing the desire for a comprehensive knowledge of things, which is something he sought himself, rather it is a desire for knowledge that does not have any end in view. Because of this,

---

[19]Ibid., 10.1.3.
[20]Ibid.

the curious person is constantly "carried away"[21] by their desire and has a "ravenous appetite"[22] for any and all knowledge that titillates. The only direction given to the desire for knowledge is the roaming of a restless self.[23]

Our desires for both pleasure and stimulation, then, involve us in constant engagement outward with created things. One result is that we rarely, if ever, pursue solitude; we won't take time out from our busyness to seek some peace and quiet and engage in self-examination. Often what we may think of as leisure or rest, Augustine would characterize as one of these forms of busyness that foreclose the possibility of solitude. Further, these desires also fail to attend to or recognize limits outside of the desire itself, and so precious grounds for self-examination are rejected.

There is still another crucial way in which lust of the flesh and lust of the eye are inimical to solitude, particularly the solitude in which we dwell alone in God's company. In the second chapter we saw that Augustine depicts our conscience as an inner space. If we are troubled over some wrong we have done, which we may be attempting to deny to ourselves, then our conscience is like a cramped apartment we share with a nagging spouse. If, on the other hand, we are frequent in examining ourselves and confessing when we have done wrong, then our conscience is a quiet, restful space of retreat, like a comfortable home, an intimate bedroom, or a desert retreat. Within that roomy inner space we can engage in dialogue with ourselves before and with God.

A bad conscience is not the only way to make our inner space feel claustrophobic. Frequently, when analyzing the results of a distorted love of the world, Augustine details how our memory is affected. One wonder of our minds is that it makes images of the outer world, so we can represent some feature of the world to ourselves when thinking. When the desire for pleasure and stimulation govern our lives, Augustine thinks that our memory becomes full of nothing but what has or will satisfy those desires.

---

[21]Ibid.

[22]Ibid., 10.2.4.

[23]For a more extended treatment of Augustine on curiosity, and an exploration of its contemporary relevance, I highly recommend Paul Griffiths, *Intellectual Appetite: A Theological Grammar* (Washington, DC: Catholic University of America Press, 2009).

He refers to how our soul "drags the deceptive semblances of bodily things inside, and plays about with them in idle meditation ... so in its private avarice it is loaded with error and in its private prodigality it is emptied of strength."[24] The "error" Augustine has in mind concerns the tremendous capacity our memories have to arrange and rearrange these representations. This is the source of human creativity, which is an undeniable good, as it is an essential way in which we are not merely determined by our experiences but can engage with our memories in order to form judgments and tell stories. Yet that same capacity for transcendence over what we remember also means that we can fantasize and persuade ourselves that our fantasies are reality. Our images of material things, which Augustine characterizes as "figments, drawn in by the bodily senses from the appearances ... of bodies" mean that it is "the easiest thing in the world to commit them to memory as they are received, or to divide or multiply them, or contract or extend them, or arrange or shuffle them or mould them in any way you like in thought."[25]

One fantasy is particularly devastating to our sense of ourselves. If our "inside" is no more than a repeated or exaggerated version of an "outer" life of pleasure and stimulation, then we may not recognize that we are images of God made for communion with God. In particular, we may fail to see that we have within us a built-in place of solitude where we can dwell alone in the presence of God. Augustine describes how when a soul "finds delight in bodily shapes and movements" then it brings them inside itself and it "wraps itself in their images which it has fixed in the memory."[26] Our inner room is crowded, in other words, with the images we have made of what gives us pleasure or stimulation; and we think that there is no space inside us. Thus even if we turn within, we are

---

[24]The Trinity, 12.3.15.
[25]True Religion, 10.18. Augustine likely has in mind here especially the Manichaeans, a Christian sect he belonged to for a decade, but eventually renounced and spent the rest of his life criticizing. They believed that the world as we know it is the result of a cosmic battle between two warring gods and that human beings are caught in the middle and needed to play a key role in restoring harmony. Though he has the Manichaeans in mind, his point does not only concern them; the propensity to fantasize in such a way that we distance ourselves from the way things really are does not, alas, belong only to this early Christian sect.
[26]The Trinity, 12.3.14.

inundated with the same people and objects that we find outside. As a contemporary teacher of Christian prayer, Martin Laird, puts it, when we turn inside we tend to replay "internal videos" that certainly don't give us a renewed sense of God's presence, quite the opposite.[27] One devastating consequence of the relentless pursuit of pleasure and stimulation for Augustine, then, is that even if we take a break from our busyness and get some time to ourselves, we may not recognize that we always have within ourselves a roomy space where we may dwell with God.

I hasten to add that Augustine does not think that, simply by turning within, we should be able to instantly clear away the images of things and behold God's presence within us. Even if we get a glimmer of that presence occasionally, Augustine thinks it will be fleeting. He believes that God's action in history includes a myriad of ways in which God gradually draws us back into relationship with God in and through the material world. Chief among these are the Son's taking on flesh in the incarnation and the various practices of the church that make use of the good of creation, such as baptism and Eucharist. In addition, as we saw in the second chapter, Augustine believes that others' lives may serve as embodied communications of God's goodness and serve to instruct and inspire us. All this is to say, the life of the church exists to orient us toward beholding God in more easily accessible, and therefore remedial, ways. While Augustine does think that eventually this will involve beholding God within as an intimate presence to our minds, this is the fruit of long-term healing. Solitude, among other practices, is one means of that healing.

Pride of life: Desire for domination

The final form of busyness is, to Augustine's mind, the most pervasive and destructive. It is "pride of life," which is derived from pride as love of one's own power. "Pride of life" is a particular

---

[27]See Laird, *Into the Silent Land: The Practice of Contemplation*, 21. Laird draws on a wealth of Christian resources, including Augustine, to offer a lucid and practical introduction to how we can lessen the internal noise within so we may begin to behold God's presence within us.

form pride takes in which we pursue others' recognition of our superiority. He describes such pride, for instance, as the "appetite for celebrity and excellence and all the vain pomp and pride of this world"; its spiritual source is the desire to be like God apart from God, establishing oneself as "the one and only, if that were possible, to whom all things are subject, in perverse imitation, that is to say, of almighty God."[28] This kind of sin, too, tends to prevent solitude. It does so, first, because we depend on the company of others for our sense of ourselves. We are constantly at work in the world, doing what we can to earn the recognition of others, so that we can establish our value in their eyes, often by asserting ourselves over them. The desire for others' approval, which we have discussed in the second and third chapters, belongs to this category of busyness. And, second, this sin specifically prevents us from dwelling alone before God because even when we withdraw from others' company, we are still engaged in commentary on them; instead of turning our attention to ourselves, to critically examine ourselves in dialogue with and before God, we keep up incessant comparisons with, and condemnations of, other people. This focus on others does not consist in interrogating ourselves about our love for them but is an interior pursuit of domination over them.

Pride of life takes a variety of forms, but all of them seem to assume that the world is like a giant market, where we need to engage in buying and selling in order to establish our worth. Augustine sees this dynamic at work in the story of the traders in the temple, who were physically removed by Jesus.[29] For these traders, and the human tendency they represent, everything is "up for sale."[30] The source of all value comes from transactions, and so the traders are engaged in endless selling. This is not just a career but a means of justifying their existence. And so they constantly "flatter themselves about their own activity" and use their works as "a matter for boasting."[31] Anything that cannot be bought and sold, like God's love, is rejected by them; to receive anything as a gift would be to extinguish their very source of self, and so the more

---

[28]*True Religion*, 45.84.
[29]Mt. 21:12-17; Mk 11:15-19; Lk. 19:45-48; Jn 2:13-16.
[30]*Homilies on the Gospel of John*, 10.6.
[31]Augustine, *Expositions of the Psalms (51–72)*, trans. Maria Boulding (New York: New City Press, 2001), 70.18.

they define themselves in terms of their work, the more they "recoil from grace."[32] Borrowing the imagery from his contemporary marketplaces, Augustine describes how each seller sets up his stall, cries aloud about the bargains he has on offer, and does his best to outshine the competition.[33] Such work is not a means to realize some good or other; it is instead a restless busyness that comes from the need to assert oneself in the world. Such traders must constantly be engaged with others—buying and selling—in order to secure their self-worth; for these people, any break from the market is only a means to go back better rested. The company of these traders is contrasted with the company of God who gives "free of charge."[34]

One particular form that pride of life may take is criticism of others, which relates directly to a focus of this book, the work of moral self-criticism. For Augustine, judgment is a role that belongs to each of us; above all, as we saw in Chapter 2, exercising our moral responsibility for ourselves involves engaging in ongoing self-criticism in order that we might acknowledge wrongdoing and work to do better. Augustine believes that the New Testament clearly teaches that Christians are accountable to one another, and so if one Christian judges that another has done wrong, she has a responsibility to speak with the other. Numerous roles in society necessarily involve judging others, such as judges, politicians, teachers, and parents. For people in these roles, judgment is a means of maintaining order and also exercising care for other human beings.[35] Yet Augustine also believes that much of the criticizing of others that we do, whether it is communicated to anyone or kept to ourselves, is unnecessary and doesn't achieve any good. As we shall see, he even suggests that criticizing others can be a rather transparent means of changing the subject from one's own faults and frailties. If we are constantly busy criticizing others, even when

---

[32]Ibid.
[33]*Homilies on the Gospel of John*, 10.6.
[34]Ibid.
[35]See, for example, *Our Lord's Sermon on the Mount*, 1.20.66; *Letters*, 104 and 265. Judgment serve what Augustine refers to as "correction" (corrigere). For a fuller consideration of this topic in Augustine's thought, see Vittorino Grossi's entry on "Correction" in *Augustine through the Ages*, ed. Allan D. Fitzgerald (Grand Rapids, MI: Eerdmans, 1999).

we are apart from others' company, we will not use our solitude for genuine self-examination before God.

Before turning to Augustine's analysis of judging others, a literary case study will serve to give us a concrete, contemporary example. The psychological and spiritual forces at work in our tendency to judge others are vividly depicted in George Saunders's short story "Puppy."[36] It is a tale of two mothers: Marie, who has emerged from what she regards as a dismal childhood of neglect to become a wife and mother of a happy (in her opinion) family; and Callie, who struggles with poverty and with a son with an intellectual disability. These two mothers are brought together because Marie's children want a puppy and Callie's family is selling one.

Marie's entire identity is an example of what Augustine refers to as pride of life and in particular the role that criticizing others can play. She defines herself in terms of her superiority to others, primarily as a parent. She is superior to her own parents, she thinks, because of the laughter that suffuses her relationship with her children and husband; she seems to take this as the ultimate sign of their love for one another.[37] As readers, Saunders invites us to call Marie's perception into question. For example, when Marie is speaking to her son while he is playing a video game, he reaches out to her and knocks her glasses off her face. Marie's presentation of this as a playful, loving gesture is hard to believe (presumably he was trying to get her to shut up) and raises further doubt about her other perceptions of herself and her family.[38] The source of Marie's misperception is her constant comparison of herself to others in order to assert her superiority as a mother.

Yet despite the fact that being a mother is so crucial to Marie's self-understanding, she repeatedly distances herself from Callie and instead identifies herself with Callie's son, Bo. In that identification, she pictures Bo as a neglected and mistreated child, as she believes herself to have been. Marie's identification with Bo means that she sets herself up further in opposition to Callie. Marie's image of

---

[36]George Saunders, "Puppy," in *Tenth of December: Stories* (New York: Random House, 2013).

[37]Ibid., 32.

[38]Ibid., 34.

herself as a great mother depends on finding foils, and Callie fulfills that role perfectly.

Over the course of the story, both mothers have a moment of solitude in which we witness their reflections on themselves. These moments reveal that the story is a modern-day updating of Jesus's parable of the Pharisee and the tax-collector; the Pharisee thanks God that he is superior to the tax-collector, whereas the tax-collector asks for God's grace.[39] Marie uses her solitude to tell God how glad she is to have her life sorted out and surmounted the struggles she encountered. She presents herself to God as someone who can share grace with others, rather than needing grace herself.[40] By contrast, Callie's solitude involves honest evaluation of her faults and deliberation about how she can love her family members better. Callie hits upon a working definition of love in her moment of solitude: "Love was liking somehow how he was and doing things to help him get even better." This seemingly simple definition of love indicates the transformative results of Callie's solitude, results that depend on Callie's focus on her own faults, rather than spending her time alone comparing herself with others or condemning them.[41]

Augustine sees a similar dynamic at work in another New Testament story involving the Pharisees, John chapter eight. In this story, the Pharisees are attempting to trap Jesus by forcing him to follow the Old Testament law for adultery, which is stoning, or to let her off, in which case Jesus would seem to be disregarding the law. Augustine identifies the Pharisees' motivation as the "pride of persecutors."[42] This is a particular form that the distorted love for domination may take, as denouncing others can earn us recognition of our superiority over them. Jesus shifts the Pharisees' focus to their own moral health. Jesus's response spares the woman's life without disregarding the law, and, most importantly, it also calls into question the Pharisees' claim to be her judges. Augustine describes Jesus's response as "questioning the questioners" and "judging the judges."[43] In so doing, he writes that Jesus is acting as God so often does by

---

[39]Lk. 18:9-14.
[40]Ibid., 35.
[41]Ibid., 42–43.
[42]*Letters (100–155)*, trans. Roland Teske (New York: New City Press, 2003), 153.4.11.
[43]*Sermons (1–19)*, trans. Edmund Hill (New York: New City Press, 1990), 13.4.

"stamping out the pride of one who seeks to punish a wrongdoer."[44]
Justice requires that the Pharisees ought to be as exacting in their
self-criticism as they are with the woman. Further, Augustine believes
that Jesus is prompting the Pharisees to recognize their own need
for compassion, so that they will in turn be more compassionate to
this woman. Any time one human being judges another, Augustine
writes, we have a case of "equal judging equal, human judging
human, mortal judging mortal, sinner judging sinner."[45]

Most importantly for us, Augustine identifies the Pharisees as
displaying an incoherent relationship between their inner and outer
selves: "Outwardly, you see, they were lying; inwardly, they failed
to examine themselves; they were looking at the adulteress, they
had no eyes for themselves."[46] The metaphor of seeing, a continued
concern in this inquiry, is very powerful here: the Pharisees are
constantly looking outwardly at others' faults, and so they are not
seeing themselves accurately. Judging others is a form of busyness
that involves moral criticism, but always with others as the target.
Augustine believes Jesus's strategy is to invite the Pharisees to dwell
in solitude before God and take their own lives as the subject of
interrogation. So, Augustine writes, Jesus's questioning of the
Pharisees "pricked [their] consciences" and they gave up wanting to
stone the woman because they were "restrained by conscience."[47]
To avoid falling into the trap of always looking outward at others'
faults, and disregarding ourselves, Augustine advises: "Let each
of you examine himself, enter into himself."[48] As we saw in the
last chapter, for Augustine self-examination in solitude helps us to
love others better. When we withdraw from judging others to judge
ourselves, we are forced to acknowledge our own neediness. An
ongoing practice of self-criticism, Augustine believes, may alter the
nature of the judgments we make of others because an awareness of
our own neediness will connect us with others. Further, Augustine
also believes that in our self-criticism we will recognize our own
need for compassion from God and others, and so we may be better
practiced at being compassionate when we engage with others.

---

[44]*Expositions of the Psalms (99–120)*, 102.11.
[45]*Sermons (1–19)*, 13.4.
[46]*Homilies on the Gospel of John*, 33.5.
[47]*Sermons (1–19)*, 13.4.
[48]*Homilies on the Gospel of John*, 33.5.

Conclusion

By way of conclusion to this chapter and to this book, we return to Jesus's practice of solitude and Augustine's interpretation of it. Augustine sees in Jesus's temptations in the wilderness, which we considered in the first chapter, our three kinds of busyness. Each of Satan's temptations invites Jesus to abandon his solitude to partake in a distorted love of the world: to turn stones into bread corresponds to the desire for physical pleasure; to throw himself down so angels would catch him corresponds to the desire for stimulation; and to worship Satan in order to rule over the kingdoms of the world corresponds to pride of life. Augustine believes that Jesus's responses to these temptations provide us with an example of how to resist distorted love of the world: "Why did he permit himself to be tempted, if not to teach us to resist the tempter?"[49] In each case, Augustine sees Satan as offering a form of busyness by which Jesus is tempted to define himself in terms of outward action in the world. We see Satan's strategy most clearly with the temptation to curiosity. Augustine paraphrases Jesus's response thus, "I won't tempt God … as though I would belong to God if I performed a miracle and wouldn't belong to him if I didn't."[50] Jesus does absolutely have the capacity to perform miracles, but he refuses to do so for the sake of proving himself to Satan. Satan wants Jesus to use his power in ways contrary to God's purposes for Jesus. Augustine writes:

> For no really holy being takes pleasure in his own power, but rather in the power of [God] from whom he receives the power to do whatever he can appropriately do; and he knows it is far more effective to be bound to the Almighty by a devout and dutiful will than by his own will to be able to do things that overawe those who cannot do them.[51]

Jesus is without pride and therefore he does not have any need to experience his own power through pleasure, stimulation, or

---

[49]*Sermons (273–305A)*, 284.5.
[50]*Homilies on the First Epistle of John*, 2.14.
[51]*The Trinity*, 8.5.11.

domination. He can resist Satan's temptations because he is well practiced at dwelling alone with and before God in solitude.

In the first chapter, I argued that Jesus's teaching on solitude has a decidedly social end in view: Jesus wants his followers to practice being different kinds of selves in private before God, so they can act differently in public. As we saw in the second chapter, Augustine inherits and interprets this teaching with his depiction of the inner space of conscience. When we withdraw into that space, and enter into dialogue with and before God, we may gain an alternative perspective on who we are that supports the work of self-criticism. A particular focus of that self-criticism, as was discussed in the third chapter, is whether we love our fellow human beings as equals. In this chapter, we have seen that the love of our own power is a further barrier to our developing an ongoing practice of self-criticism in solitude before God. If we constantly want to experience our own power through acting outwardly in the world, then we will never pause and turn inward to critically interrogate ourselves. Further, each of these forms of busyness depends on a mastery of other creatures that does not attend to our given limits. The love of our own power can lead us to fail to attend to the relationships that define us as creatures, which should inform how we act.

A recurring theme of this book was the connection between solitude and forgiveness. Jesus instructs his followers to pray these words in their solitude: "Forgive us our trespasses, as we forgive those who trespass against us." Augustine argues that self-examination in the privacy of conscience before God may make us more rigorous in our self-criticism and so more sensitive to our need for forgiveness. And awareness of our own need for forgiveness may help us to be more compassionate toward others, giving us grounds to reach out in solidarity with those whom we might otherwise be quick to condemn. In one of his sermons on Jesus's temptations, Augustine offers another insight into the relation between solitude and forgiveness. He suggests to his listeners that Jesus's ability to resist Satan's temptations prepares him to so astoundingly request forgiveness from God for those who crucify him. Augustine argues that lessening our need to experience our own power is the crucial way to increase our ability to forgive others. When you do not love your own power, you cannot only resist constant busyness, you can even persevere in "gentleness" when others betray you and hate you.[52] Not needing to demonstrate or experience one's own power, then, prepares one to refuse vengeance. The pursuit of vengeance is an especially easy option if we busy ourselves constantly by seeking domination over others. To be wronged by another is a delicious opportunity to lord it over them, to self-righteously eke out whatever recognition of my superiority I can, including by judging the one who wronged me. To retreat regularly into solitude, and to pursue God's company alone there, is to practice being a self who receives identity from God's companionship, rather than needing to assert one's value in competition or rivalry with others. Thus, we return to a theme we have pursued at length in this book, beginning with Jesus and continuing with Augustine's interpretation of Jesus's solitude: dwelling alone before God in private may help us to love better in public.

---

[52]*Sermons (273–305A)*, 284.5.

BIBLIOGRAPHY

Translations of Works by Augustine

The Advantage of Believing. Translated by Ray Kearney. In *On Christian Belief*, edited by Boniface Ramsay, 116–154. New York: New City Press, 2005.

Answer to Faustus, a Manichean. Translated by Roland Teske. New York: New City Press, 2007.

The Catholic Way of Life and the Manichean Way of Life. Translated by Roland E. Teske. In *The Manichean Debate*, edited by Boniface Ramsey, 28–103. New York: New City Press, 2006.

The Christian Combat. Translated Robert P. Russell. In *Writings of Saint Augustine*, vol. 4, edited by Ludwig Schopp, 315–353. New York: CIMA Publishing, 1947.

City of God (Books I–X). Translated by William Babcock. New York: New City Press, 2012.

City of God (Books XI–XXII). Translated by William Babcock. New York: New City Press, 2013.

City of God. Translated by R. W. Dyson. Cambridge: Cambridge University Press, 1998.

Confessions. Translated by Maria Boulding. New York: New City Press, 2007.

The Excellence of Widowhood. Translated by M. Clement Eagan. In *Treatises on Various Subjects*, edited by Roy J. Deferrari, 279–319. New York: The Fathers of the Church Inc., 1952.

Expositions of the Psalms (1–32). Translated by Edmund Hill. New York: New City Press, 2000.

Expositions of the Psalms (33–50). Translated by Maria Boulding. New York: New City Press, 2000.

Expositions of the Psalms (51–72). Translated by Maria Boulding. New York: New City Press, 2001.

Expositions of the Psalms (121–150). Translated by Maria Boulding. New York: New City Press, 2004.

On Genesis: A Refutation of the Manichees. Translated by Edmund Hill. In *On Genesis*, edited by John E. Rotelle, 39–104. New York: New City Press, 2002.

Homilies on the First Epistle of John. Translated by Boniface Ramsey. New York: New City Press, 2008.

Homilies on the Gospel of John. Translated by Edmund Hill. New York: New City Press, 2009.

Letters (1–99). Translated by Roland Teske. New York: New City Press, 2001.

Letters (100–155). Translated by Roland Teske. New York: New City Press, 2003.

Letters (156–210). Translated by Roland Teske. New York: New City Press, 2004.

The Literal Meaning of Genesis. Translated by Edmund Hill. In *On Genesis*, edited by John Rotelle, 168–506. New York: New City Press, 2002.

The Lord's Sermon on the Mount. Translated by Michael G. Campbell. In *The New Testament I and II*, edited by Boniface Ramsey, 23–114. New York: New City Press.

Miscellany of Eighty-Three Questions. Translated by Boniface Ramsey. In *Responses to Miscellaneous Questions*, edited by Raymond Canning, 27–157. New York: New City Press, 2008.

Sermons (1–19). Translated by Edmund Hill. New York: New City Press, 1990.

Sermons (20–50). Translated by Edmund Hill. New York: New City Press, 1990.

Sermons (51–94). Translated by Edmund Hill. New York: New City Press, 1991.

Sermons (94A–147A). Translated by Edmund Hill. New York: New City Press, 1992.

Sermons (145–183). Translated by Edmund Hill. New York: New City Press, 1992.

Sermons (184–229Z). Translated by Edmund Hill. New York: New City Press, 1993.

Sermons (230–272B). Translated by Edmund Hill. New York: New City Press, 1993.

Sermons (273–305A). Translated by Edmund Hill. New York: New City Press, 1994.

Sermons (341–400). Translated by Edmund Hill. New York: New City Press, 1995.

Teaching Christianity. Translated by Edmund Hill. New York: New City Press, 2014.

The Trinity. Translated by Edmund Hill. New York: New City Press, 1991.

True Religion. Translated by Edmund Hill. In *On Christian Belief*, edited by Boniface Ramsay, 29–104. New York: New City Press, 2005.

Works by Others

Alison, James. *Raising Abel: The Recovery of the Eschatological Imagination*. London: SPCK, 1997.

Arendt, Hannah. *The Life of the Mind, Volume One: Thinking*. New York: Harcourt Brace Jovanovich, 1977.

Arendt, Hannah. *The Origins of Totalitarianism*. 2nd edn. New York: Meridian Books, 1958.

Austen, Jane. *Mansfield Park*. 1814. New York: Penguin Books, 1996.

Ayres, Lewis. *Augustine and the Trinity*. Cambridge: Cambridge University Press, 2010.

Berkowitz, Roger. "Solitude and the Activity of Thinking." In *Thinking in Dark Times: Hannah Arendt on Ethics and Politics*, edited by Roger Berkowitz, Jeffrey Katz, and Thomas Keenan, 237–245. New York: Fordham University Press, 2010.

The Book of Psalms. Translation and commentary by Robert Alter. New York: W.W. Norton & Company, 2007.

Cary, Phillip. *Augustine's Invention of the Inner Self*. Oxford: Oxford University Press, 2000.

Clausen, Ian. "Seeking the Place of Conscience in Higher Education: An Augustinian View." *Religions*, 6 no. 6 (2015): 286–289.

Deresiewicz, William. "The End of Solitude." *The Chronicle of Higher Education*, January 30, 2009, http://chronicle.com/article/The-End-Of-Solitude/3708.

Deresiewicz, William. "Solitude and Leadership." *The American Scholar,* Spring 2010, http://www.theamericanscholar.org/solitude-and-leadership/print/.

Dideberg, D. *Saint Augustin et la premiere epitre de saint Jean.* Paris: Editions Beauchesne, 1975.

Dodaro, Robert. "Between the Two Cities: Political Action in Augustine of Hippo." In *Augustine and Politics,* edited by John Doody, Kevin L. Hughes, and Kim Paffenroth, 99–116. New York: Lexington Books, 2005.

Eliot, George. *Middlemarch.* 1871. New York: The Modern Library, 2000.

Gregory, Eric. *Politics and the Order of Love: An Augustinian Ethic of Democratic Citizenship.* Chicago: University of Chicago Press, 2010.

Griffiths, Paul. *Intellectual Appetite: A Theological Grammar.* Washington, DC: Catholic University of America Press, 2009.

Grossi, Vittorino. "Correction." In *Augustine through the Ages,* edited by Allan D. Fitzgerald. Grand Rapids, MI: Eerdmans, 1999.

Haflidson, Ron. "Imitation and the Mediation of Christ in Augustine's *City of God.*" *Studia Patristica,* 18 no. 70 (2013): 449–455.

Hanby, Michael. *Augustine and Modernity.* New York: Routledge, 2003.

Harris, Micahel. *Solitude: In Pursuit of a Singular Life in a Crowded World.* New York: Thomas Dunne Books, 2017.

Hirshfield, Jane. *Ten Windows: How Great Poems Transform the World.* New York: Alfred A. Knopf, 2015.

Johnson, Fenton. "Going It Alone: The Dignity and Challenge of Solitude." *Harper's Magazine,* April 2015: 31–40.

Kenney, J. P. *Contemplation and Classical Christianity.* Oxford: Oxford University Press, 2013.

Laird, Martin. *Into the Silent Land: The Practice of Contemplation.* Oxford: Oxford University Press, 2006.

Maitland, Sarah. *How to Be Alone.* London: MacMillan, 2014.

Markus, Robert. *Saeculum: History and Society in the Theology of St. Augustine.* Cambridge: Cambridge University Press, 1970.

Mathewes, Charles. *A Theology of Public Life.* Cambridge: Cambridge University Press, 2008.

Milbank, John. *Theology and Social Theory: Beyond Secular Reason.* Oxford: Blackwell Publishers, 1990.

The New Oxford Annotated Bible, edited by Michael D. Coogan. New Revised Standard Version. Oxford: Oxford University Press, 2010.

Nietzsche, Friedrich. *The Gay Science*. 1882. Translated by Josefine Nauckhoff. Cambridge: Cambridge University Press, 2001.

O'Donovan, Oliver. *The Desire of the Nations: Rediscovering the Roots of Political Theology*. Cambridge: Cambridge University Press, 1996.

O'Donovan, Oliver. *Ways of Judgment*. Grand Rapids, MI: Eerdmans, 2005.

Plotinus. *The Enneads*. Translated by George Boys-Stones and edited by Lloyd P. Gerson. Cambridge: Cambridge University Press, 2018.

Prufer, Thomas. "Creation, Solitude and Publicity." In *Recapitulations: Essays in Philosophy*, 32–34. Washington, DC: Catholic University of America Press, 1993.

Ramsey, Boniface. "Introduction." In *The Lord's Sermon on the Mount*, edited by Boniface Ramsey, 11–16. In *The New Testament I and II*. New York: New City Press, 2014.

Robinson, Marilynne. *Gilead*. New York: Farrar, Straus and Giroux, 2004.

Saunders, George. "Puppy." In *Tenth of December: Stories*. New York: Random House, 2013.

Sorabji, Richard. "Graeco-Roman Origins of the Idea of Moral Conscience." *Studia Patristica*, 44 no. 44 (2010): 361–383.

Sorabji, Richard. *Moral Conscience through the Ages: Fifth Century BCE to the Present*. Chicago: University of Chicago Press, 2014.

Taylor, Charles. *Sources of the Self*. Boston: Harvard University Press, 1992.

Thoreau, Henry David. *Walden and Civil Disobedience*. 1854. New York: Penguin Books, 1960.

Turkle, Sherry. *Reclaiming Conversation: The Power of Talk in a Digital Age*. New York: Penguin Press, 2015.

Turkle, Sherry. *Alone Together: Why We Expect More from Technology and Less from Each Other*. New York: Basic Books, 2011.

Turner, Denys. *The Darkness of God: Negativity in Christian Mysticism*. Cambridge: Cambridge University Press, 1998.

Verheijen, Luc. "The Straw, the Beam, the Tusculan Disputations and the Rule of Saint Augustine—On a Surprising Augustinian Exegesis." *Augustinian Studies*, 2 no. 2 (1971): 17–36.

Webb, Melanie. "'On Lucretia who slew herself': Rape and Consolation in Augustine's *De ciuitate dei.*" *Augustinian Studies* 44, no. 1 (2013): 37–58.

Williams, Rowan. "Politics and the Soul: A Reading of *The City of God.*" *Milltown Studies* 19, no. 12 (1987): 55–72.

Williams, Rowan. "Has Secularism Failed?" In *Faith in the Public Square*, 11–22. New York: Bloomsbury, 2012.

INDEX